·THOMAS R. KEYES·
·DAVID MILLER·

THE GLOBAL INVE$TOR

HOW TO BUY STOCKS AROUND THE WORLD

Longman Financial Services Publishing
a division of Longman Financial Services Institute, Inc.

While a great deal of care has been taken to provide accurate and current information, the ideas, suggestions, general principles and conclusions presented in this book are subject to local, state and federal laws and regulations, court cases and any revisions of same. The reader is thus urged to consult legal counsel regarding any points of law—this publication should not be used as a substitute for competent legal advice.

Executive Editor: Kathleen A. Welton
Project Editor: Ellen Allen
Interior Design: Mary Kushmir
Cover Design: Anthony Russo

© 1990 by Thomas R. Keyes and David Miller

Published by Longman Financial Services Publishing
a division of Longman Financial Services Institute, Inc.

Printed in the United States of America
90 91 92 10 9 8 7 6 5 4 3 2 1

Library of Congress Cataloging-in-Publication Data

Keyes, Thomas R.
    The global investor : how to buy stocks around the world / by Thomas R. Keyes and David Miller.
        p.   cm.
    Includes index.
    ISBN 0-88462-914-7
    1. Stocks.   I. Miller, David.   II. Title.
HG4661.K38   1990   89-12586
332.63'22—dc20   CIP

CONTENTS

041359

NOTE: The charting software used to prepare the illustrations throughout this book carries only three digits at this size, thus dropping the final zero or zeros in most cases.

DEDICATION

To the Fathers
Donald M.
and
John S.

ACKNOWLEDGMENTS

This enjoyable venture began when Bill Rini introduced me to Fred Dahl, who was full of questions. The book is an answer to those questions.

General information came from many people, such as Stefano Miari of Milano, Italy, who was my student in southern France preparing to sell securities in Monte Carlo while awaiting full convertibility of the Italian currency. New York Stock Exchange (NYSE) personnel helped by arranging visits to the floor of the exchange with Wayne Randall and Sandi Schroeder. Other security exchange personnel have gone out of their way to help. At the Vienna Bourse, the office of the president provided a most enjoyable and knowledgeable English-speaking guide. Frank McAuliffe of the National Association of Securities Dealers (NASD) always knew where to locate tough-to-find information.

Colin Meredith assisted by constantly asking "Is that important?" Any redundancy remaining in the text is there in spite of Colin.

In the middle of the Minneapolis winter, the furnace repairman restored our heat and brought a little light besides. Having recently read that eight of the ten largest banks in the world are Japanese, he wanted to know why and thought we were just the people to tell him—and to forecast the future of trade between the U.S. and Japan. Why is it, we wondered, that those who write about investing are thought to possess special insight into the future?

Though we have no crystal ball, we do have computers,

and they have been essential in gathering and organizing information. Equally essential were the people who made the computers perform their magic. Pat Brady and John Keyes prepared spreadsheets and answered continuous questions about that marvelous tool. Prassana "Ray" Uppalari and Kerry Keyes kept the computer systems operating. Creating the book would have been impossible without the help of these individuals.

I owe thanks to others who helped in special ways:

To that small group who continually share information with me about events in the world of global investing, and who were the book's first readers. These include Jerome West, Cate Brady, Teresa Keyes, and John Keyes.

To Bill Kemp, who compared accounting and tax systems of the United Kingdom (U.K.) and Japan for me.

To Chris MacLennan, who introduced me to MetaStock.

To Cate Brady, who researched many of the databases for me.

To Giorgio Botteon, whose conversations added insight.

To Larry Skjei, who shared some of his worldwide investment experiences with us.

To Suzanne Proctor, who helped me understand.

To William Cameron and MarketBase Inc., Research Technology Corporation of Australia, Warner Computer Systems Inc., and Lotus Information Network for the data used in our stockmarket and currency charts.

And, finally, to my coauthor David Miller, who made this project so enjoyable.

PREFACE

A nonfiction book is one side of a conversation, the writer's side. It contains, the writer hopes, answers to all the questions that readers would ask were they present to hold up their end of the discussion. Rarely is a book as close as this one to the questions it attempts to answer. Each chapter, in fact, was taken from one or more questions Fred Dahl asked coauthor Tom Keyes.

At the time, Fred was an editor at a publishing company in New York. He and Tom were discussing the possibility of a book on another subject. As the conversation progressed, Tom kept referring to events in Europe and Asia when explaining his view of U.S. stock market history — say, on Black Monday. Fred was irked by the apparent circumlocution and said something like "I don't understand why people are always talking about German interest rates and the Japanese investor's view of the dollar and the like. World news doesn't have any affect on U.S. stock prices, does it?"

"Look what happened on the Sunday before Black Monday," Tom said. "James Baker has a press conference and announces that the Germans have told him they won't lower their interest rates to help their economy grow. That means the mark will rise in value and the dollar will continue falling. And if the Germans are determined to take actions that will drive the dollar down, Baker says, the U.S. may respond by driving it down even further. His statements make front-page news in Europe, and investors there dump U.S. stocks on overseas markets. The slaughter begins before Wall Street is open for business on Monday morning. Difference in time zones, you know." In expanded form, that's chapter 1 of this book.

"But what's all this talk about owning foreign stocks?" Fred responded. "I can't call up my broker and buy Japanese stocks, can I?"

"Depends on the firm," Tom said. "Is it one of the big three here in New York?"

"Yes, as a matter of fact. But my representative doesn't know anything about foreign stocks."

"Probably not," Tom agreed. "But he can get you stocks on foreign markets just the same. I have a friend who's been trading Australian stocks for years. He even has a bank account in Australian dollars. Anyway, you can buy some foreign stocks that trade right here in the U.S. as American Depositary Receipts. Or you can get into mutual funds that buy foreign stocks." That's the gist of chapter 2.

"Hold on," Fred interjected. He was irked again. "I don't see the relevance of Australian dollars and German marks and yen and so forth. I don't have to worry about the value of yen unless I visit Japan, right? And how often am I going to do that in my lifetime? Twice maybe?" Segue into chapter 3.

"Fred," Tom said patiently (Tom seldom gets irked, especially not when he has a good audience), "the stocks are priced in yen. But you can't spend yen in the U.S. When you sell the stock, you get yen that you have to exchange for dollars. What if the value of the yen drops while you own a stock? The yen from your stock sale won't be worth as many dollars as when you bought the stock. Not that yen have been dropping much lately. Which is one reason Japanese stocks have been so good to U.S. investors."

"Okay, okay," Fred said. "I have to worry about yen. But how do I go about actually purchasing a foreign stock?"

"Well, there's some questions you ought to ask your rep," Tom advised. "You want to know how soon the trade settles, for example. It takes a lot longer in some places than the five days required in the U.S. You want to ask about commissions if you go through a foreign broker. You probably want to know about the round lot size in the foreign market. That sort of thing." The rest of the questions to ask your rep are in chapter 4.

"Let's say I buy a foreign stock, then. What can go wrong?"

No doubt Tom laughed at that question. He has a distinctive, booming, infectious laugh—a sort of fringe benefit for those who work with him. "Everything can go wrong," of course. "Just as in the U.S. Only you have some different pitfalls to look out for—like buying stock in a company that gets nationalized. Or buying stock in a country that suddenly becomes the target of a U.S. embargo." These and other things that can go wrong are illustrated by the stories in chapter 5.

"So how do I go about choosing a country?" Fred inquired. "How do I avoid those pitfalls?"

"For one thing," Tom answered, "look at the fundamentals. Of course, sometimes information is in a language you can't read. And accounting assumptions are a little different from country to country. Look at the P/E ratios in Japan, for example. They might be three or four times what they are in the U.S., but the Nikkei Index keeps right on climbing. Drives U.S. analysts nuts." Other fundamentals to consider are covered in chapter 6.

"Is there some other way to choose?" Fred wondered.

"Sure," Tom said, reassuringly. "Use the charts. Do a little technical analysis. Try not to buy when the market's up so high it's likely to crash, for instance. Or when a stock price goes up suddenly for no good fundamental reason. In some markets that's a sign of manipulation." You can read about charts in chapter 7.

"Sounds like other markets are a little different from ours. How do foreign markets work?"

One can imagine another laugh at this point, and a response something like "They don't, always. But then neither does ours. All markets are manipulated, by the way." And that probably was followed by a bit of market history, an explanation of the way markets compete for your investment business. It's all in chapter 8.

"How do I get information to make decisions about buying and selling?" Fred asked, obviously less irked and more enthusiastic than at the beginning.

"I've been getting some of it through my computer," Tom said. "And there are some magazines and books."

You'll find a great deal of current information throughout this book and in the appendices. Illustrations in the text are drawn from Tom's database. Most of it comes from the U.S. Commerce Department. If you're puzzled by the numbers, it's probably because the Commerce Department recalculates price data with 1968 values as a baseline. So the numbers don't always correspond to values you're used to from familiar indexes. Percent changes in prices are the same, though, so the graphs are fine for illustrating points about the market.

The charts in Appendix 1, on the other hand, come directly from the indexes of various markets. In part this discrepancy is due to a positive development: as we wrote the book, more data became available. You can begin your own search for up-to-date information by consulting the electronic sources listed in Appendix 4 and the books and periodicals included in the Bibliography.

Oh yes. Fred's final question: "I think you'd better write the book on foreign stocks before the one we started discussing. Don't you?"

PART I

THE GLOBAL MARKETPLACE

CHAPTER 1

World News and
Your Portfolio

Perhaps your newspaper has a special section called "Global Report" or "The World in Brief," or, simply, "World News"— as if there were U.S. news on the one hand and world news on the other. We want to divide events, it seems, into those that affect our lives, and those that affect others without affecting us. So many of our families came here, after all, to escape from somewhere else. We muscled out the Spanish, the French, the British. President Washington told us to beware of entangling alliances. We still like to think we're going it alone over on our side of the ocean—building our own cars, sewing our own clothes, investing in our own industries.

But our independence from the world is a myth—a powerful and dramatic tale that oversimplifies reality. Our horizons are much wider than we care to admit. Other nations are much closer. October 19, 1987, brought that reality home to us with a resounding crack in the market. A crack that truly was heard around the world.

By Monday evening, we realized that markets around the world had gone down hand in hand, like lovers leaping together from a bridge. The morning of the 20th, and the rest of the mornings for several weeks, we listened to news about the Japanese and other market on our car radios (radios that were invariably Japanese as, frequently enough, were the cars). The Nikkei Index, which measures performance on the Tokyo exchange, approached the Dow Jones Industrial Average (DJIA) in visibility. And no wonder. Their profiles suddenly seemed remarkably similar. We began to sense those connections between world markets. Look at the similarities in figures 1–1 and 1–2, which are graphs of the DJIA and the Nikkei Index. Figure 1–3, the Hangseng Index, shows Hong Kong's market suffering the same fate. Figure 1–4 shows the International Stock Exchange (ISE) in London climbing a similar slope and crashing over the same peak, and figure 1–5 shows the market in Canada taking a similar ride. Clearly, we are not alone as investors. What happens in the United States is tangled up with events in Asia and the European Community and the rest of the Americas.

The sound of many markets crashing in unison was bound to wake us up to reality. But the real shocker may have been the fact that the DJIA started the day on that Monday 200 points below the close of Friday the 16th. We had to ask what had been happening on the weekend. And of course it wasn't gremlins invading the floor of the NYSE. It was investors all around the world trading U.S. stocks on other exchanges in response to continuing bad news— world news or U.S. news, as you wish.

Treasury Secretary James Baker, you may remember, was slugging it out with the Germans over economic issues. He thought it high time the Germans lowered their interest rates to kick-start the European economy. The Germans, on their side, were afraid such policies would lead to inflation. Furthermore, they thought it just about time we raised our interest rates if we wanted to attract foreign investors to dollar-denominated securities.

In response to that idea, Baker took to the radio on

Figure 1–1. The DJIA through Black Monday

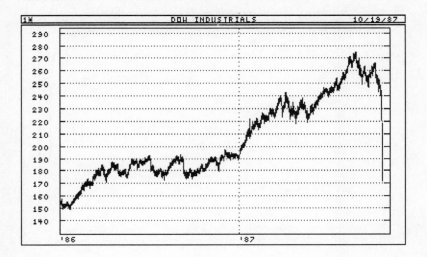

Figure 1–2. Japan: Through Black Monday

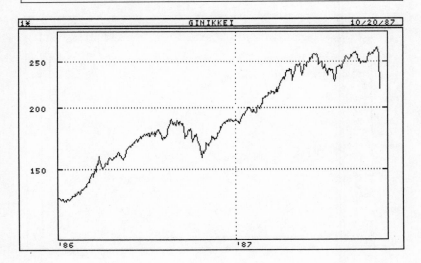

5

Figure 1–3. Hong Kong's Hangseng Index through Black Monday

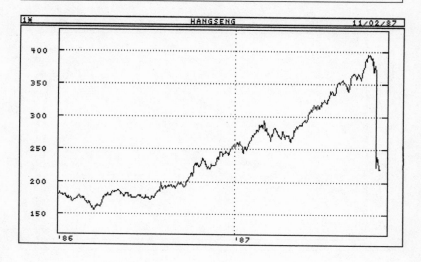

Figure 1–4. London's ISE through Black Monday

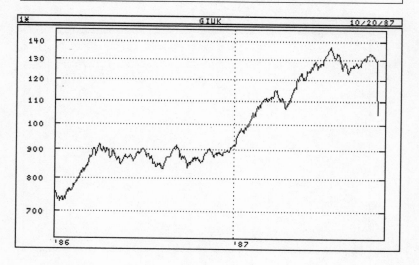

6

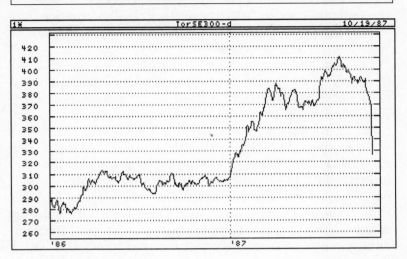

Figure 1–5. Canada's Toronto Exchange through Black Monday

Sunday, October 18, to announce that he would rather let the dollar drop out of sight than raise interest rates. Big investors around the world took that as a sign to bail out of U.S. securities—because a falling dollar is bad for corporate profits, and what's bad for the bottom line hurts dividends and stock prices. And they could do that because U.S. stocks trade all around the world, not just in U.S. markets, and because London and Amsterdam and Zurich and Tokyo and Singapore and Melbourne are all ahead of us on the world clock. While we were sleeping Sunday night, our securities were getting beat up on three continents and several islands.

But it was hardly the first time that the world markets had demonstrated their togetherness. In 1974, for example, our stock market hit bottom simultaneously with a host of other markets around the world. In 1929, one national market after the other slid into chaos—London in June,

7

Paris in July, the United States in October. In 1720, for that matter, the French Mississippi scheme went belly up about the same time as the bursting of the British South Sea bubble. In figures 1–6 to 1–9, you can see clearly the worldwide impact of the recession in 1974.

Financial disaster is a global empire. We see this, occasionally, and forget. Soon enough we're looking around for local demons. Program trading, for example, or portfolio insurance, or the low margin requirements for futures contracts. Every crash has its villain. In 1974 it was the specialists. Even President Kennedy took a turn as market scapegoat—in 1962 when he jawboned the steel industry into price rollbacks. In 1929 we grumbled about bear pools and short selling. Our scapegoats help us forget about Europe and Japan and international currency markets and foreign interest in our national debt and the web of relationships that affect U.S. stock prices.

So much for the lessons of history. We are perhaps no more willing now to admit our ties to the world than we were in the past. But the ties are there—and growing ever tighter. Electronic communications are shrinking the world daily. A century ago, events in one country might have taken months to affect markets elsewhere. Now what happens in Bonn or Tokyo moves U.S. stock prices before we wake up to hear the news. But our computers never sleep. They were watching, with electronic eyes, on Saturday and Sunday before Black Monday. They watched U.S. blue chip stocks keep falling in price on exchanges outside the United States. And, as if by magic, they showed the market down on Monday morning when we were trying to call our brokers. Our faithful computers were telling us that U.S. stocks were trading overseas, and a growing number of foreign stocks were trading in the U.S. They were telling us that world news is U.S. news and has an immediate bearing on the worth of our

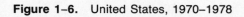

Figure 1–6. United States, 1970–1978

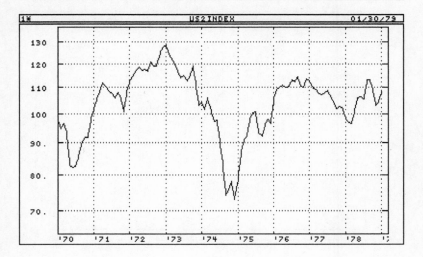

Figure 1–7. Canada, 1970–1978

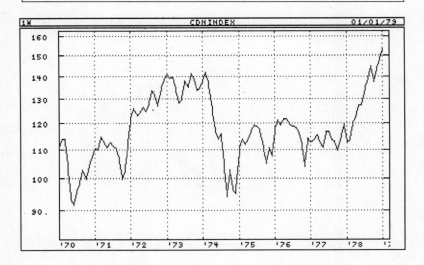

Figure 1–8. United Kingdom, 1970–1978

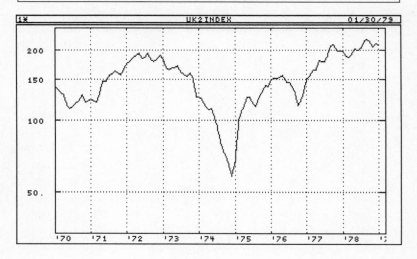

Figure 1–9. West Germany, 1970–1978

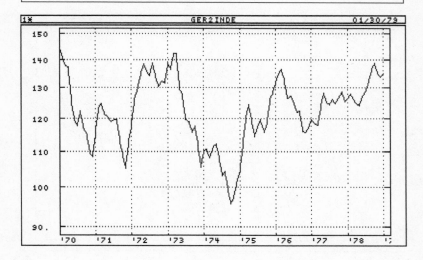

retirement funds, college savings programs, and nest eggs, on our mad money and on our cautious money as well. We are international investors already, whether we will it or not.

Made in America?

Actually, we've become international investors the way we became international consumers. Put on your Reeboks and walk to your nearest General Motors (GM) dealer if you need convincing. Look at the new Geo line, consisting of barely camouflaged Toyotas, Suzukis, and Isuzus. Hike on over to your Ford dealer for a look at the XR4Ti—made in Germany. Raise the hood of a Taurus. Some of them have engines designed by Yamaha Corporation (Yamaha), the Japanese motorcycle manufacturer. Drive a Mercury Tracer—they're made by Mitsubishi. Take a look at a Chrysler lot. Test drive a Dodge Colt or Chrysler Conquest—more Mitsubishis. Is this what the commercials mean by "Born in America again"?

Are these cars American? German? Japanese? What nationality is a car of Japanese design produced in a Japanese-owned facility in Kentucky? What is a Ford Probe, built in Michigan by Mazda Motors (Mazda)? How do we cope with the idea that the Japanese are building Hondas in the United States and importing those cars into Japan? This is not, you understand, meant as an argument against buying homemade products, just as indication of the direction the wind is blowing. "Made in America" is no longer a simple concept. Perhaps it never was. "Made in Japan" isn't either. There is a great deal of unpleasant rhetoric issuing from corporations and governments on both sides of both oceans, but it's accompanied by a surprising amount of cooperation. Sometimes we sound like bitter enemies, sometimes like fast friends. Families are a lot like that, and perhaps the shrinking of the world is simply revealing to us the primal family ties that bind us all together.

Global Markets or Global Market?

There is nothing simple about the global marketplace. As we've seen, markets in the industrialized economies tend to rise and fall together. There is also a tendency for the lesser-developed economies to move in similar directions. But these are not ironclad laws. Even when markets rise and fall in unison they may move along the same slopes at different rates. In fact, this lack of complete synchronicity creates investment opportunity for the internationally minded. The following charts illustrate some of the diversity of the global markets. As you can see from figures 1–10 to 1–13, the recovery from Black Monday was anything but uniform — with the Japanese market far outperforming the United States, United Kingdom and Canada.

The charts are telling us that the world is still diverse: we don't have one unified global market at this point. Instead, we have a host of markets with overlapping borders. This is exactly why we have the opportunity now to become global investors. Other markets are close enough that we can begin to understand them, follow their cycles, and invest in the securities listed there. As Chrysler Corporation (Chrysler) engineers pursue joint ventures with Mitsubishi Motors Inc. (Mitsubishi) and Ford Motor Company (Ford) with Yamaha, individuals can buy shares in foreign corporations. In fact, how foreign are the corporations that are setting up factories in our country and sending the products home to their own countries? How domestic are auto manufacturers that buy their electronic components overseas and hire foreign companies to redesign their engines? The United States, after all, is an amalgam of all the world's people. Why shouldn't your portfolio be equally diverse?

12

Figure 1–10. Japan, 1987–89: Black Monday and Beyond

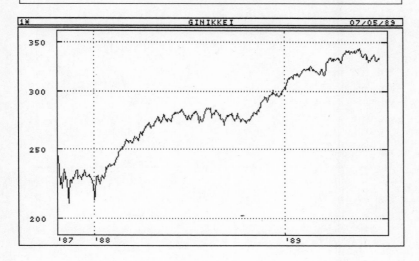

Figure 1–11. U.S., 1987–89: Black Monday and Beyond

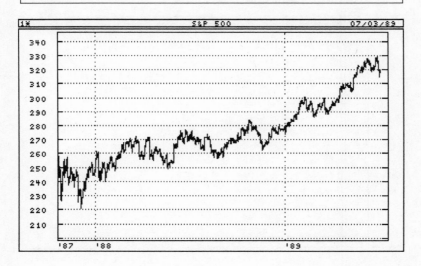

13

Figure 1–12.   Canada, 1987–89: Black Monday and Beyond

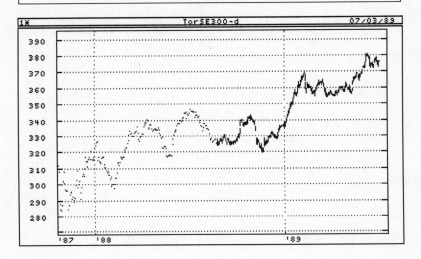

Figure 1–13.   U.K., 1987–89: Black Monday and Beyond

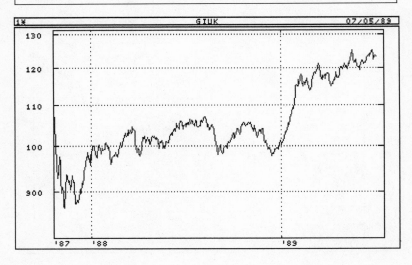

Conclusion

We can lament the shrinking of the globe. Or we can adapt. In the chapters that follow you will find a celebration of the expansion of investment horizons. Many financial advisers now believe that a portfolio without international equities is insufficiently diversified. We agree. And we write here about the special risks involved in foreign investing too. Explorers need to be especially cautious, no question about that. But this is an optimistic book, which, we think, makes it as essential to pessimists as it is congenial to optimists.

Understanding international markets is, of course, a reward in itself. Following foreign stocks may make you more wealthy, if you're astute and fortunate in your investment choices. It may also make you less wealthy. But it will, without doubt, make you richer in awareness and provide you with a fund of fascinating stories to tell. On your way to choosing and keeping track of a foreign portfolio, you will gain insight into the larger world we Americans often seem eager to ignore.

International finance is as intriguing for the window-shopper as for the investor. And it provides a window on the world. The fluctuating prices of securities reflect the flow of trade from nation to nation, the making and losing of vast fortunes, the struggle for improved living conditions, the drama of war and revolution, and, in general, all the earthly aspirations of humanity. Anyone who loves to travel or just to read the *National Geographic* is a candidate to become an international market-watcher. For all who would be observers or investors, then, the following chapters provide a guidebook for an adventure we hope you will find enriching in every way.

CHAPTER 2

Four Ways to Become a Global Investor

To buy or not to buy foreign stocks is no longer the question. Rather you should be asking how much to buy and how to do it. We believe foreign stocks should make up at least ten percent of your portfolio. The value of diversifying internationally is too compelling. And there are simply too many attractive foreign equities available for you to ignore them all. In fact, as you grow more familiar with foreign markets you may want more than ten percent of your portfolio invested outside the United States.

Not that U.S. markets don't provide a vast number and variety of stocks to choose among. For that matter, U.S. stocks themselves provide a degree of international diversification—think of those automobile stocks discussed in chapter 1, for example. Nevertheless, the U.S. market includes far less of the world's total equity activity than in the past, even in the recent past.

In 1984, for example, the total value of stocks in all the world's markets was a bit over $2.9 trillion. U.S. markets made up about 54 percent of that amount, Japanese markets about 21 percent, U.K. markets about 7.5 percent. By 1988, world market capitalization topped $11 trillion—about 29 percent of which was Japanese, 25 percent of which was U.S., and about 24 percent of which was British. The U.S. market is still growing, but our wedge of the world pie is narrowing rapidly.[1]

Granted, then, that an increasing fraction of the world's stock opportunities lies outside the U.S. marketplace. And granted that 10 percent of each investor's portfolio should be composed of foreign stocks. One still has to know how to choose. So this chapter describes four pathways into international investing: foreign shares trading in foreign markets, foreign shares trading in the United States (usually as American Depositary Receipts [ADRs]), investment companies holding foreign stocks, and U.S. multinationals. Selecting from these alternatives, you can diversify your portfolio, open the door to sometimes dramatic gains in overseas markets, and not step over your risk threshhold.

We'll begin with a brief look at direct purchase of foreign shares—brief because the rest of the book concentrates on foreign markets, so there's no need to go into great detail here. After that abbreviated journey into foreign markets, we'll look at domestic foreign stocks you can purchase in U.S. markets—as ADRs or in the portfolios of mutual funds and closed-end investment companies.

Foreign Shares, Foreign Markets

The most adventuresome way to accumulate foreign stocks is to buy them directly in foreign markets. Doing so is rather like buying a foreign car overseas—a Jaguar, let's say. With the Jaguar, you have to contact the dealer, get the car shipped to the United States, pay costs incurred in that process, be certain you comply with relevant U.S. regulations, and learn to drive with the steering wheel on the right side of the car. But for various reasons, saving money among them, you may be more than willing to undergo those nuisances rather than simply buying the Jaguar here and letting the importer deal with the headaches.

In somewhat the same way, buying stocks in foreign markets is typically more difficult and more costly. Depending on the country, your inconveniences may include language and other communications problems, thin markets, outdated clearing systems, restricted currency exchange, unrestricted insider trading, very different accounting assumptions, or some combination of the above. You also may face higher commissions, withholding of foreign taxes, and fees for various services rendered by various financial institutions. But if you really want the stock, you'll overlook the difficulties—because you think you have a chance at being more than adequately rewarded.

Actually, the problems vary considerably from place to place. If it's a Canadian stock you want, for example, there may be little or no difficulty. Quite a few Canadian companies are registered with the Securities and Exchange Commission (SEC) to trade on U.S. Exchanges and over-the-counter. You'll find, for example, Alcan Aluminium, Ltd., Canadian Pacific Limited, and about twenty other Canadian equities listed on the NYSE. Many U.S. broker-dealers are members of Canadian exchanges. Canadian laws and taxes are not unfavorable to U.S. investors. And all information about the stocks is published in English— except in Quebec.

Things are not quite so cozy in other English-speaking markets, such as the United Kingdom, Australia, New Zealand, Singapore, Hong Kong, and South Africa. For one thing, they're overseas. Distance makes a difference, even in this shrinking world. We are separated by an ocean and several time zones, after all. And we have different cultures—meaning different feelings about regulating investment markets, and different ways of keeping books. Still, we have much in common, and the language is not

19

a problem, or not an insuperable one. (English does undergo transformations from country to country.)

Outside the English-speaking world, the difficulties tend to mount. Japan, in some ways, is an exception. There are large broker-dealers there, such as Nomura Securities International, Inc. (Nomura) that are familiar with the United States. Indeed, Nomura has branches in this country and underwrites U.S. government securities offerings. The Japanese financial system is strongly influenced by the U.S. model—though significant differences exist. A good deal of information on Japanese markets is readily available in English-language publications. Yet Japanese accounting is quite different from ours, and that can make it difficult for us to interpret their markets. As we'll see in chapter 8, for example, western analysts are quite puzzled by Japanese price-earnings ratios (P/E ratios), which are routinely three to four times as high as P/E ratios in the U.S. markets.

Not all Asian markets are so hospitable. In Korea, for example, the potential U.S. investor is up against all sorts of challenges—not the least of which is a government prohibition against unauthorized foreign investment in the stock market. At present, the only available equity for individual investors is a government-approved closed-end investment company: The Korea Fund, Inc., which trades on the NYSE. (We'll discuss that opportunity in the section of this chapter on investment companies.) If you want to buy shares in large, profitable Korean companies such as Hyundai Electronics, Inc. (Hyundai), Gold Star Electronics International, Inc. (Gold Star), Korean Airlines and Samsung Electronics, Inc. (Samsung), you're out of luck. This aggravates a good many investors, who consider South Korea a likely candidate for "the next Japan." Some observers believe the Roh Tae Woo government will soon take down the barriers to foreign investment. But for the present, it's the Korea Fund or nothing.

Other markets similarly limit or exclude foreign

investment. Taiwan stocks are available through a closed-end fund. Thailand, another candidate for the Japan of the future, puts quotas on foreign stock ownership. The quotas fill up rapidly and the foreign shares of desirable companies trade at a premium. There is also a Thai Fund and it, too, trades at a premium. But markets in many countries are open to foreigners, and the major stumbling blocks for individual investors are unfamiliarity and the undeniable nuisances of foreign investing. Investors who brave the vagaries of the Australian market may be unwilling to trade in, say, Germany or Italy simply because they are uncomfortable with the prospect of receiving investment information in a foreign language. But that's a cultural problem, not a market problem.

Despite the obstacles, a growing number of U.S. investors experience the adventure and financial reward of investing in such places as the United Kingdom, Germany, Italy, Scandinavia, Japan, Australia, New Zealand, and Mexico. In 1986, for example, U.S. investors put $80 billion into foreign stocks—up from a mere $4.25 billion in 1976.[2] They were attracted by the chance to diversify their portfolios. They knew that some other markets were soaring above the DJIA—Mexico's exchange was up 700 percent before the crash in '87; Tokyo, as we saw in chapter 1, recovered from Black Monday much faster than the United States. And they were aware that other currencies were growing stronger at the expense of the dollar—thus multiplying stock market gains for investors. And they were aware that many of the world's great publicly traded corporations are now based outside the United States.

For now, that's enough said about direct foreign investment—which is the subject of all the chapters in part 2. The rest of this chapter is a brief detour into more domestic matters—ADRs, mutual funds, closed-end funds, and domestic multinational corporations. These, too, are part of the international investment arena. Though they are closer to home and more easily accessible, still they partake of the risks and peculiarities of foreign markets.

ADRs: American Depositary Receipts

U.S. investors who would rather not undertake the adventure of overseas investing can find dozens of foreign stocks trading right at home on the NYSE, American Stock Exchange (Amex), and National Association of Securities Dealers Automated Quotation System (NASDAQ). Representing economies as diverse as the United Kingdom and the Netherlands Antilles, Spain and Zambia, Finland and Japan, most of these stocks trade in the form of ADRs. As of 1987, 97 ADRs traded on NASDAQ, 34 on the NYSE, and five on the Amex. Another several hundred were listed in the Pink Sheets that circulate between market makers.

So what is an ADR? It is a negotiable receipt for shares of stock deposited in a bank. In the usual case, a broker-dealer buys shares in a foreign stock and leaves them with a bank in the issuer's country. A correspondent bank in the United States then creates the ADRs, which trade in the U.S. marketplace in lieu of the stock. In some cases, one ADR represents one share of stock. In others, the ADR represents a number of shares (one Isuzu Motors [Isuzu] ADR, for example, equals five shares of Isuzu stock).

There is nothing alien about trading ADRs. Buying Jaguar ADRs, for instance, is no different from buying shares of Apple Computer Inc. (Apple) or any other over-the-counter (OTC) stock. The investor phones in an order, buys and sells in U.S. currency, and receives dividends in dollars. The bank holding the shares of stock takes care of such nuisances as currency exchange and withholding of foreign taxes. The investor follows the ADR's price in the NASDAQ daily listings.

We compared buying foreign shares in foreign markets

to purchasing cars overseas. ADRs are the financial ana-
logs of imported cars: though they come from other countries, they have been modified in the appropriate ways to
conform to U.S. regulations. And they are available at your
local supplier, priced in your currency, and not subject to
higher commissions, fees, or taxes.

Just the same, not all ADRs are created equal. Some,
for example, are registered with the SEC; others are unregistered. Registration means disclosure of relevant information. Failure to be registered does not, however,
necessarily indicate something negative about an ADR. The
registration requirement wasn't passed until 1983, and it
isn't retroactive. ADRs trading before that time were grand-
fathered into exempt status, and these unregistered companies include such high-profile giants as Fuji-Photo Film
Inc. (Fuji Film), Toyota, Nissan Motor Corp. (Nissan), and
the Hong Kong and Shanghai Banking Corporation.

Another significant distinction among ADRs is whether
they are sponsored by the issuing company. If sponsored,
the ADR confers voting rights and the issuer provides the
investor with proxies and annual reports. Unsponsored
ADRs, created by a bank without the issuer's cooperation,
don't include voting privileges. Those who hold them don't
receive annual reports or proxies. Lack of sponsorship, like
absence of SEC registration, does not imply that the
security is second-class in any way. In fact, Toyota, Nissan,
and Fuji Film are unsponsored as well as unregistered.

One caveat is in order here. Though ADRs are traded
in U.S. dollars, their prices reflect conditions in the home
country—such as the exchange value of the foreign
currency in dollars. The price of Schlumberger Ltd.
(Schlumberger) ADRs, for example, will tend to rise and
fall with the guilder (assuming no change in the price
of Schlumberger in guilders). The price of Cadbury
Schweppes, Inc. (Cadbury) ADRs will move with the pound,
and the value of Norsk Data SA (Norsk Data) will alter with

23

the kroner-to-dollar exchange rate. As an investor following Schlumberger, Cadbury, or Norsk Data in your newspaper, you'll want to keep track of currency exchange rates.
Chapter 3 of this book shows you how to do that, in one
relatively painless lesson.

Next let's look at investment companies—a way to get
into foreign markets without having to select particular
stocks. Instead, you let the fund's professional money manager make the tough decisions—and have most of the fun.

Investment Companies

Investment companies come in two varieties: open-end and
closed-end. Open-end investment companies, better known
as mutual funds, constantly issue and redeem shares. If
you want to invest, you buy shares from the company.
Whenever you want to sell, the company buys from you.
But there is no secondary trading. Closed-end funds, in contrast, raise all their investment capital in an initial offering, after which the shares trade like common stock on an
exchange or over-the-counter. Both mutual funds and the
less familiar closed-end companies are involved in foreign
securities markets. Their advantages and disadvantages
differ significantly, as we'll see in the upcoming discussion.

Generally, investment companies with foreign holdings
follow one of three strategies. A country fund invests only
in one country. An international fund is free to buy any
stock that isn't U.S.-based. A global fund leaves its money
managers free to select investments from any country, foreign or domestic. International and global portfolios, such
as Fidelity's Magellan Fund and the Templeton Growth
Fund, are almost entirely of the open-end variety. Country funds, like The Korea Fund, Inc. and The Mexico Fund,
Inc. are almost all closed-end.

Investment companies can be a very attractive option

for investors who want to get into foreign markets but prefer to delegate stock selection to a professional money manager. In addition to professional management, investment companies provide diversification—most in a global fund, least in a country fund. Combining your limited resources with those of other investors allows you to own a piece of many securities, thus reducing your risk of losing a lot of money on any one selection.

To help you decide which of these types of funds, if any, suit your needs, we will consider the advantages and disadvantages of each in turn—starting with funds that invest in one country.

Country Funds

Perhaps through travel, business contacts, the news, or general reading, you've become fascinated by another country. You've been to Paris, Milan, or Madrid to trace the European roots of American culture. A visit to Australia has brought you in touch with a land whose pioneer heritage resembles ours. Business ventures have put you in awe of the phenomenal growth and energy of Japan, South Korea, or Thailand. Perhaps studies of your family tree have made you aware of ancestral ties to these or other countries.

Your enthusiasm inspires you to invest. Then you realize you don't know any particular companies well enough to choose wisely. Or the country limits foreign investment. Maybe you don't know the language and you're worried about your ability to follow events affecting your investment. So a country fund seems like just the ticket. There are funds investing solely in Japan, Korea, Thailand, India, Mexico, Brazil, Spain, Italy, France, Germany, and Sri Lanka (Ceylon)—to name a few of approximately two dozen examples. Virtually all of these country funds are closed-end investment companies that trade on the NYSE and are quoted daily in your paper.

The Korea Fund provides a good example. In 1988, one might have become interested in Korea for one of several reasons. The advent of a new government under Roh Tae Woo might be taken as a harbinger of either positive or negative changes in the economy—depending on one's politics. The Olympic Games, held in South Korea in September, provided many non-Koreans with their first sustained look at the country since the demise of the MASH television series (which hardly whetted one's appetite for things Korean). Hyundai automobiles, Gold Star electronics, Samsung radios, and Sojin pianos were rapidly increasing their visibility in overseas markets. As of mid 1989, however, there was only one way to act on the impulse to invest in Korean stocks: the Korea Fund. Fortunately for those interested in Hyundai, Gold Star, and Samsung, the fund was heavily invested in those corporations.

Like most country funds, the Korea Fund is a little short on track record. Established in 1983, it's actually one of the older funds. Most of the others are children of the later part of the decade. Like almost all the country funds, it trades on the NYSE. You can look up its per-share price, just like that of any other publicly traded company, in the exchange listings. But you may also want to look up its price weekly in *Barron's*, in the section devoted to closed-end funds. There you'll find both the market price of the fund and the net asset value of its portfolio. (Net asset value [NAV] is the market value of fund assets—cash as well as securities—reduced by liabilities.) And you'll find this information most interesting—since the two values are often quite different. On occasion, the market price of the Korea Fund has run as high as 150 percent over the net asset value. This premium reflects the popularity of the fund as the only vehicle allowing entry into a popular market. In the following *Barron's* clipping, you can see that the Korea Fund was trading at a premium of 87.15 percent on April 17, 1989.[4]

26

Table 2-1.

Fund Name	Exch.	NAV	Price	% Diff.
H&Q Healthcare Inv	NYSE	8.88	$7\frac{1}{4}$	− 18.36
Hampton Utils Tr Cap-b	AMEX	9.48	$8\frac{3}{8}$	− 6.38
Hampton Utils Tr Pref-b	AMEX	48.5144	$\frac{9}{16}$	− 8.14
Helvetia Fund	NYSE	10.77	$9\frac{3}{8}$	− 12.95
India-f	NYSE	13.19	$9\frac{5}{8}$	− 27.03
Italy Fund-b	NYSE	9.78	$8\frac{1}{2}$	− 13.09
Korea Fund	NYSE	17.90	$33\frac{1}{2}$	+ 87.15
MG Small Cap	NYSE	9.50	$8\frac{1}{8}$	− 14.47
Malaysia Fund	NYSE	10.58	$8\frac{1}{2}$	− 19.66
Meeschaert G&C	MWST	z	z	z
Mexico Fund-b	NYSE	8.97	8	− 10.81

In buying above the net asset value, investors may seem to be running a substantial risk. If South Korea opens the market to foreign investment, the fund's market price will probably move closer to net asset value. In the meantime, however, the fund may pay off handsomely if the underlying portfolio continues to gain in value and the premium doesn't drop.

Trading above net asset value is not typical of country funds, nor of closed-end investment companies in general. Most trade at a discount. The Brazil Fund, at this writing, is trading at almost a 40 percent discount. The Mexico Fund, as you can see in the preceding *Barron's* chart, is trading at a 10.81 percent discount, which represents a substantial narrowing. The Mexico Fund has been discounted by 30 percent and more. The funds invested in European countries, such as France, Italy, and Germany, tend to trade at discounts as well.

In an obvious sense, discounted funds are bargains — and occasionally one reads of increased investor interest in them for that reason. The situation is undeniably tempting. Let's say you buy a fund at a big discount. Then the country's market prospers, raising the values of securities in your fund. Seeing the improvement, other investors rush to buy the fund and the discount diminishes — or, as with the Korea Fund, turns into a premium. You could be a double winner, gaining both on increases in the portfolio's value and on decrease in the discount.

Naturally, the downside risks are magnified in just the same proportion as the upside potential. Let's say you buy the Transylvania Fund at a discount of 10 percent. The net asset value might be 20, for example, and the market price 18. Rumors suddenly arise that the fund manager, Count Dracula, is about to be charged with insider trading, and this scandal coincides with a general market collapse. As everything in the portfolio heads south, the net asset value declines from 20 to 16. Worse, the discount widens from 10 percent to 25 percent, knocking the market price down to 12. You've been a double loser.

Country Funds and Their Markets

Take a look at figure 2–1, a chart of the Mexico Fund. You can see how its price movement gave investors a taste of the Mexican market's extreme volatility.

You can see that the Mexico Fund was a very poor investment if held from mid 1982 through 1986, when both the U.S. stock market and the dollar were on the rise. Though the fund went up with the U.S. bull market until mid 1983—starting at a bottom of 2 and reaching a high of 5, it then went down to 2 again during the next two and a half years. In 1986, however, it began climbing again, and in 1987 shot straight up—from around 3 at New Year's to over 14 by October, a rise of almost 400 percent in less than a year! But then, with marvelous symmetry, it went right back down to 3 by the end of December. In 1988, the fund recovered to around 6 in December—far below its peak before the crash in 1987, well below its value in 1981.

Which brings us to another noteworthy feature of country funds. Although they may be composed entirely (or mostly) of the stocks of one country, their performance

Figure 2–1. The Mexico Fund, 1981–1989

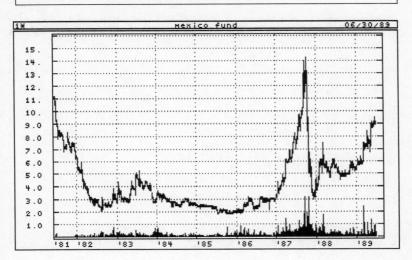

doesn't mirror only the performance of the underlying securities — much less of the market as a whole. An investment like the Korea Fund or the Japan Fund also reflects U.S. investors' views of the Korean market or the Japanese market. In figures 2–2 through 2–4, for example, you can see that the chart of the Japan Fund's performance in late 1987 and 1988 looks much more like the chart for the DJIA than the chart for the Nikkei Index.

This sort of performance might disappoint an investor who bought into the Japan Fund to profit from the strength of the stock market in Tokyo — especially since Japanese stocks are directly available to the U.S. investor either through the Tokyo exchange or as ADRs. The lesson is a familiar one: what you gain in comfort you give up in reward potential. With a country fund you gain the comforts of professional management and diversification, but you lose the chance to participate directly — for good or ill — in the performance of particular stocks and the overall

Figure 2–2. The DJIA: Black Monday and After

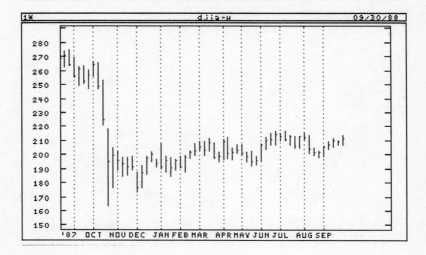

Figure 2–3. The Japan Fund: Black Monday and After

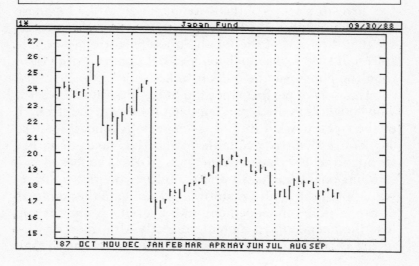

Figure 2–4. The Nikkei Index: Black Monday and After

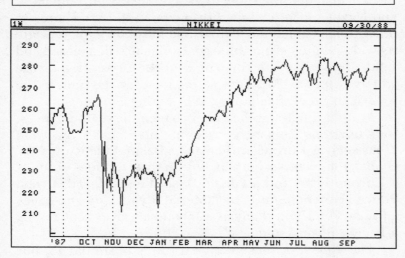

market. Still, in countries such as Korea and Thailand, the fund may be your only chance to participate at all.

Regional Funds

From the country-specific funds, one branches out into investment companies with portfolios of ever-widening geographic scope. Our first step outward is into regional funds, where we find a mixture of closed-end and open-end arrangements.

Among closed-end funds, for example, we find the Asia Pacific Fund, the Scandinavia Fund, Scudder Fund Distributors, Inc. (Scudder), New Asia Fund, and a rather interesting variation on the regional theme—the Templeton Emerging Markets Fund. Established in 1987, the Emerging Markets Fund specializes in a type of country rather than a group of countries. According to its literature, the

31

fund envisions investing in 42 emerging economies around the world, including some in Asia, Africa, South America, and New Guinea. Included in the portfolio are shares of other funds—the India, Brazil, and Mexico Funds. Despite its wide-ranging geographic goals, this is still a closed-end fund. If you like the concept, and the reputation of the widely respected Mr. Templeton, look for the fund in the American Stock Exchange (ASE) listings.

Mutual funds significantly broaden the regional investor's horizons, generally sweeping up stocks from wide areas such as Europe or the Pacific Basin. Fidelity and GT Global, for example, both include in their families of funds a Europe Fund and a Pacific Basin Fund. Merrill Lynch Pierce Fenner & Smith, Inc. (Merrill Lynch), too, manages a Pacific Fund, and Nomura, a Japanese broker-dealer, sells a Pacific Basin Fund.

The appeal of these regional funds is similar to, but not exactly like, the attraction of country funds. Because of their wider geographic boundaries, they magnify the commonly accepted benefits of investing in funds—diversification and professional management. The more territory your fund covers, the more diversification you receive and the more you need the help of a professional money manager.

If, on the other hand, you have strong investment preferences, the regional funds may look less attractive to you. To gain diversification and professional management, you give up a degree of control.

International Funds

An international fund, technically defined, may invest anywhere but at home. The terminology is confusing, so be careful. All the investment companies discussed here are international in one sense: they invest outside their home country. And you may sometimes hear the name *international fund* used that inclusively. You may also hear *international fund* used with the same meaning as *global fund*, that is, including domestic and foreign investments.

Why choose an international fund? Why turn down a promising investment, whatever the portfolio? In general, international funds are useful to balance domestic investments with a diverse foreign portfolio. Since the fund has no domestic investments, it will not be affected—not directly, at least—by U.S. political, economic, and financial conditions. This should make it something of a hedge against losses in the rest of your portfolio.

Whether this balancing act works as well in practice as it does in theory is a matter of conjecture. An article in the May 1988 *AAII Journal*, for example, questions the effectiveness of diversifying through investment in international mutual funds. As the authors point out, "to the extent that economies are becoming more integrated, diversifying among stocks in different countries may not necessarily reduce risk."[5] Ironically, they say, the same shrinking of the globe that fosters international investment may be reducing the diversity of world markets. As we all become more tightly interlinked, we tend to be affected in the same way by the same conditions. It's the lesson of Black Monday with a vengeance.

Yet though we may be a shrinking world, we are not yet one world politically, economically, or financially. Currencies still rise and fall in opposing directions. One market thrives while another languishes. Even those economies ascending or descending together may be moving at very different speeds. And—perhaps most telling—one market's calamity tends to be another market's bonanza. Rising oil prices may bring merriment in Mexico and Bahrain, but they mean misery in the U.S. and Japan. When coffee prices go up, spirits may soar in Brazil but the mood darkens in the U.S.—especially in the early morning.

In fact, even within one country's economy, conditions

affecting investment can alter in different directions or at different rates. In the 1970s and early 1980s, for example, some states in the southern U.S. enjoyed an impressive rise in population, construction, industrial growth, and national reputation that came at the expense of other regions. However small the globe may seem, it is still staggeringly diverse. A carefully selected international fund may, indeed, serve to offset fluctuations in one's domestic investments. An international fund also may attract one simply because it gives a canny manager scope to ferret out the best investment opportunities in the foreign world's most lucrative markets.

Professional management and worldwide diversification do not guarantee that a fund will prosper in general, or that it will do well when domestic investments are doing badly. Investing in a mutual fund, in other words, doesn't mean that an individual investor escapes the burden—or loses the opportunity—of making investment decisions. The investor still has choices to make. International funds must be selected on the basis of several variables: management and track record, mix of countries (and currencies), mix of industries, and mix of particular stocks.

Many of the major mutual fund families now offer international funds: Templeton, Fidelity, IDS Financial Services, Inc. (IDS), Kemper Corporation (Kemper), Scudder Fund Distributors, Inc. (Scudder), and T. Rowe Price Associates, Inc. (T. Rowe Price) are just a few examples.

Global Funds

The very essence of diversification, the global fund takes all the world as its market. Again, many of the major fund families include one or more global portfolios. You have at least a couple of dozen U.S.-based global funds to choose among.

For some, the global fund is the ultimate cop-out: "total

abdication of responsibility for your investments," as one writer puts it, perhaps tongue in cheek.[6] Others consider global funds the best conceivable use of a good money manager. There's something to be said for the latter point of view. What could make better sense than giving some of your money to a money-management genius who has free run of the world's stock markets to pick the best investments available?

But notice that you've made a number of investment decisions by the time you've gotten to this point: that worldwide is better than domestic-only, that investment company shares are better for you than direct stock investment, and that one money manager is better than another. If you're that confident in your ability to pick one fund over another, you may feel you're also able to pick one company over another—never mind whether it operates in the United States or the Pacific Rim.

Don't mistake these remarks for a bias against mutual funds, global or otherwise. Consider them instead a prejudice against complacency. In the end, your investments express your own beliefs, even if that's a belief that someone else can take better care of your money than you can.

As you make your choices, consider the record of an outstanding global fund, the Templeton Fund—named, of course, for its highly respected manager, John Templeton. Compare the fund's record with the DJIA for the decade 1978 to 1988 in figures 2–5 and 2–6. Did Mr. Templeton's fund outperform the DJIA?

Over the course of the decade, the two lines look remarkably similar. The Templeton Fund, diversified globally, rose from about 6 to about 19 on the chart—a 316 percent total appreciation, or better than 30 percent per year. The DJIA, rising from about 800 to about 2700, grew approximately 296 percent—roughly 30 percent per year. Not much difference. But the fund clearly outperformed the DJIA for long stretches. And it just as clearly

Figure 2–5. The Templeton Fund, 1978–1989

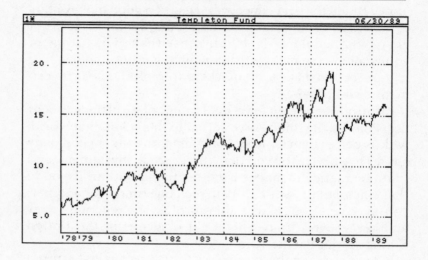

Figure 2–6. The Dow Jones Industrial Average, 1978–1989

underperformed at other times. From 1978 to 1984, for example, the fund grew from about 6 to about 13—better than 200 percent. The DJIA, during those same years, rose from 800 to around 1200—only 50 percent. From 1982 to 1987, however, the DJIA surged ahead of the fund. During those bullish years, the U.S. market rose from about 800 to about 2700—almost 350 percent. The Templeton Fund, because of its global diversification, missed out on some of the domestic glory. It rose *only* from about 8 to about 19, or less than 250 percent.

The record of the Templeton Fund is very remarkable, no question about that. Growth of 30 percent per year over a decade is marvelous to behold. But those who would rather keep closer control over their investments, perhaps selecting country funds, ADRs, or even buying stocks overseas, should take heart. If you can beat the DJIA, you may also be able to best John Templeton. That's an ambitious and tantalizing goal.

Investment Companies Outside the U.S.

Both open- and closed-end investment companies exist in countries outside the United States. In the United Kingdom and Australia, for example, investors may choose among a large number of open-end unit trusts (about 1,000 in England alone) or from a lesser number of closed-end investment trusts. Some of these trusts invest in other countries or regions of the world, including North America.

Mutual funds are an important part of the securities markets of other countries, such as Germany, Austria, New Zealand, and Israel. Technically, however, U.S. investors cannot own foreign mutual funds that aren't registered with the SEC. This means that, at the very least, you cannot buy them through U.S. brokers or directly from the fund management. In some cases they may be available if you have a foreign bank or brokerage account.

Multinationals

Chances are pretty good that you're already participating in the international economy as an investor. Do you own International Business Machines Corp. (IBM) or ITT Corp. (ITT)? Even their names suggest their international connections. As of mid 1988, 54 percent of IBM's assets were located outside the United States; and better than 63 percent of its operating profits came from foreign business. ITT's international involvement was more modest at that time: its foreign assets were just under 15 percent of the total, and its operating profits were 30 percent foreign.

For world travelers, perhaps it's just as obvious that McDonald's Corporation (McDonald's) has become international. The golden arches have become a familiar landmark for Americans traveling in Europe and Japan—where U.S.-style hamburgers were once very difficult to find. But by 1987, more than 35 percent of McDonald's assets were foreign and over 23 percent of its operating profit was generated abroad. Coca-Cola, Inc. (Coke), with 26 percent of its assets outside the United States, produced over half its revenues and almost three-fourths of its 1987 operating profit in other countries.

Nor were IBM and Coke the only large U.S. multinationals to earn more than half their operating profits outside the home country. According to *Forbes*, they were joined in that accomplishment by American International Group, Johnson & Johnson, Aluminum Company of America (Alcoa), the Gillette Company (Gillette), Mobil Corporation (Mobil), Digital Equipment Corporation, and Control Data Corporation.[7]

These are, of course, American companies. You buy their shares on the NYSE, follow their stock prices in your local paper or *The Wall Street Journal*, and receive their dividend checks in dollars. It all seems reassuringly domestic.

But the success of your investment in McDonald's, Coke, IBM, Gillette, or Mobil depends to a significant extent on whether citizens of other countries eat the right hamburgers and drink the right soft drinks, load the right software into the right computers, and fill up at the right gas stations.

Your return on such investments also is affected by the currency of the country where those foreign consumers eat their burgers, drink their Coke®s, and gas up their cars. Londoners may queue up to consume Big Mac®s and Cokes instead of kidney pie and porter. But their eating habits may not help your portfolio if the pounds they spend on those American items translate into a decreasing number of dollars. And the pound's power depends to a degree on the wisdom of the British parliament and prime minister. Your investment in many a familiar American blue-chip stock is already a global risk on the consumer habits and political vision of foreigners.

Perhaps the most telling measure of the effect of international trade on domestic stock markets is the foreign involvement of those thirty companies that make up the Dow Jones Industrials. Only a few of the thirty aren't offered on exchanges outside the United States. And many of these companies, whose collective price makes up the most-quoted indicator of U.S. stock market performance, receive a significant percentage of their revenues from foreign operations—with Exxon Corporation (Exxon) leading the pack at 75.1 percent. Table 2–1 provides a sense of how international the Dow Jones Industrials really are.

In some cases, the simple "yes" in the third column conceals as much as it reveals. The American Express Company, Inc. (American Express), for instance, trades on nine foreign exchanges—Toronto, Amsterdam, Basel, Frankfurt, Geneva, Zurich, London, Paris, and Tokyo. Simply by owning shares of the stocks included in the Dow, then, an investor diversifies in a limited way into foreign markets.

Table 2–2.

Company	Foreign Revenues	Listed on a Foreign Exchange
Exxon	75.1%	Yes
Coca-Cola	54.7%	Yes
IBM	54.0%	Yes
Merck	50.6%	Yes
Texaco	49.8%	Yes
Boeing	45%	Yes
Woolworth	42.6%	Yes
Goodyear	40.4%	Yes
Alcoa	39.6%	Yes
Eastman Kodak	39.6%	Yes
MMM	38.3%	Yes
DuPont	38.2%	Yes
Proctor & Gamble	32.5%	Yes
Union Carbide	30.9%	Yes
McDonald's	29.8%	Yes
USX	27.4%	Yes
United Technologies	27.4%	Yes
General Motors	23.0%	Yes
Chevron	22.7%	Yes
Phillip Morris	20.4%	Yes
American Express	19.8%	Yes
Allied Signal	19.3%	Yes
Westinghouse	10.4%	Yes
International Paper	10%	Yes
General Electric	9.4%	Yes
Sears	6.6%	Yes
Primerica	6.0%	No
AT&T	2.3%	Yes
Bethlehem Steel	None	No
Navistar	None	No

That's a pretty fair measure of how far into the global market the U.S. has already gone. And it's also a pretty reliable indication that individual ownership of foreign stock will increase, since individual investors—perhaps beginning with employees of companies like IBM, Coca-Cola, and McDonald's—will, no doubt, be anxious to follow down the trail broken by their multinational employers. But the point is that you've come partway down that trail already if you own stock in a U.S.-based firm with international operations. Welcome, then, through the back door, to the world of global investment!

Conclusion

We began this chapter by advising you to put at least 10 percent of your portfolio into foreign stocks. Then we looked at four ways to fill that 10 percent. Direct purchase in foreign markets is the most adventuresome of the four, with the highest potential rewards and risks. It's also the method with the most interesting future: one can only believe that the globe will continue shrinking, and that investors will continually gain easier access to more markets.

Next in directness is the purchase of foreign stocks trading in the U.S. as ADRs. About 130 such investments trade at present on an exchange or on NASDAQ's National Market System (NMS)—with hundreds of others available through OTC trading. ADRs, while not providing as many opportunities as direct investment, do save investors some of the expenses and headaches involved in foreign trading.

Investment companies appeal to investors who want diversification and professional management. They also give U.S. investors their only access to some foreign markets—Korea and Taiwan, for example.

The diversification offered by investment companies might interest a global investor for a couple of reasons. First, if you're attracted to one country, a fund that holds stocks in different industries in that country may reduce your concern about investing in a distant land. Second, you can use funds holding foreign stocks to balance your U.S. securities, especially if these funds specialize in countries that react differently than your own to world economic conditions—say, for example, countries whose currency tends to strengthen at the expense of the dollar, or countries that benefit from conditions harmful to the U.S., such as changing oil prices.

And what about professional management? This appeals to those who haven't the time, inclination, or expertise to undertake the care and feeding of their own portfolios.

The mutual fund manager is, in effect, the broker for a whole host of stock transactions that the investor never has to think about. The manager makes all the buy and sell decisions and handles all the ordinary paperwork. The investor just cashes the dividend checks (unless they are automatically reinvested in the fund) and decides when to sell the fund itself.

For investing overseas, professional management can mean relief from any number of headaches—including special accounting and tax considerations, language difficulties, and the problems of currency exchange. On the other hand, a self-confident and interested global investor may neither want nor need an investment manager. In such cases the investor will very likely be unwilling to pay for professional management, and will plunge directly into foreign stocks and foreign markets.

Speaking of the charge for professional management, mutual funds vary greatly in size and type of sales charge. Some funds take a sales charge out of the initial investment, and this initial fee can be as much as 8.5 percent of your capital. Others charge a back-end load, which reduces the amount you receive when selling the shares. Funds can also charge 12b-1 fees (named after the controversial rule that governs them). These periodic fees compensate the fund for such expenses as advertising, and they reduce the amount of the fund's assets. There are also no-load funds available—but *no load* sometimes means only no initial sales charge. In any case, investors need to be certain they know how much of their money is going into the various sorts of fees and charges. And, when it goes there. Discovering a back-end load only when you want to redeem your shares is more than a little annoying.

Finally, we looked at the most domestic method of all— buying U.S. multinational companies that have offices in other countries, trade on foreign exchanges, and make some portion of their profits from overseas operations.

Although this may feel like the back-door method of entering foreign markets, it does build some international diversification into your portfolio.

Now we return to the truly foreign side of foreign investing for a look at currency exchange—a subject that is absolutely essential to making intelligent decisions about the stocks, ADRs, or funds in your portfolio.

Endnotes

1. The 1984 figures are from *Capital International Perspective* 1985/1, Price Waterhouse, Hentson & Cie, Intersec Research. The 1988 figures are calculated from data in *Institutional Investor,* April 1988. Total world capitalization grew dramatically in part because Eurosecurities were not included before 1988. See also Appendix 3 in this book.

2. Raj Aggarwal, "International Investing: Taking the Direct Route," *AAII Journal,* February 1989, p. 8.

3. *NASDAQ ADRs: The Preferred Way to Trade* (Washington, D.C.: National Association of Securities Dealers, Inc., 1988), p. 5.

4. *Barron's,* April 17, 1989, p. 123.

5. Kenneth Jessell and Jeff Madura, "International Funds: What Factors Affect Their Returns?", *AAII Journal,* May 1988, p. 10.

6. David Smyth, *Worldly Wise Investor* (NY: Franklin Watts, 1988) p. 40.

7. *Forbes,* July 25, 1988, pp. 248–50.

CHAPTER 3

The Importance of Yen— and Other Currencies

Yen, pounds, marks, francs, lira, won, pesetas: the names of currencies are words in an exotic language. As a global investor, you will use this language when you discuss your foreign stocks. Are you buying at a low price? That depends on the value of the currency. Has your stock appreciated since you purchased it? That, too, depends on the currency and its value in U.S. dollars.

This chapter is a primer on currency and the part it plays in buying and selling foreign stocks. As a primer, it begins at the beginning. Before we're finished, you should know what the strengthening and weakening of currencies is, how currency fluctuation affects your investments in general, and how specific securities have reacted to currency changes in the real world. You will also know how to evaluate the prices of stocks denominated in foreign currencies, where to find information about currency values, and how to calculate what another currency is worth in terms of your own or a third country's. You'll even get some practice calculating exchange rates.

This is basic stuff. You have to know it. But you don't necessarily have to know it right now. You can skip this chapter if you're already comfortable converting yen into dollars, dollars into pounds, and pounds into yen. Or you might try skipping to appendix 2 for a quick refresher. This isn't a detective novel: nothing stops you from going on to other sections and saving this chapter for later—when you're evaluating prices of potential purchases, for example. Consider this as a short training program and a reference. For most of us, currency exchange is puzzling and requires occasional relearning.

Of Currency and Equity

For Europeans, the existence of diverse currencies is just another fact of life. But for Americans (U.S. citizens, that is) currency exchange is exotic—perhaps a once-in-a-lifetime experience. We scarcely ever see another country's money—except the occasional Canadian coin, which we pass along at face value. So we don't have to trouble ourselves, as citizens of other nations do, about conversion of one currency into another.

Even if you do not yet own foreign stocks, however, money is an essential part of the world news, and, as we showed in chapter 1, world news affects your portfolio. When other currencies gain or lose international buying power, the dollar's value changes accordingly; and that, in turn, alters the U.S. trade balance. And the trade balance is one of those factors that move the stock market. In 1987 the value of the dollar in relation to Japanese yen and German marks was an important ingredient in the heartbreak of Black Monday.

To take a less global perspective, let's say you do own Japanese stocks. As the yen goes, so goes the value of your Japanese investments—other factors being equal. The yen strengthens; you grow richer. The yen weakens; you grow poorer. The same is true for the pound and your British investments, the mark and your German stocks, and so on. Furthermore, the impact of the exchange rate on your net worth is quite a separate issue from the market value, in the home country, of your stocks. British Petroleum Company P.L.C. (British Petroleum) might not move a pence in price while you own it (theoretically, anyway). But the stock's value to you, in your own currency, will vary with the exchange rate.

When you buy a foreign stock, then, your investment has two parts: equity ownership and currency speculation. Let's say, for example, that you save a sum of money to invest in stock. When the time comes to buy, you narrow your choices to a Japanese stock and a U.S. stock in the same industry—automobiles, for example. Imagine (unlikely as it may seem) that the two automobile stocks seem about equal in value—but you suspect the yen is about to gain in strength against the dollar. In those circumstances, the Japanese stock looks like the better investment— strictly because of the increasing value of the yen.

So why not just speculate in the currencies themselves? It's possible to do, after all. Money is a commodity, something you can buy and sell, like pork bellies or grain. If you like, you can go to the nearest money-center bank and exchange your dollars for yen or marks or pounds at the current exchange rates. You can then hold the foreign money in an account and keep an eye on the exchange value. At least you can do so if you're reading this in January of 1990 or afterward, the date the Federal Reserve Board (FRB) will allow U.S. banks to begin opening foreign currency accounts.

Let's say the yen/dollar exchange rate is 135 yen per dollar, and you trade $100 for 13,500 yen. You bank the yen and wait. Three months later their value has increased to 120 per dollar. (There's one of the confusing things about currency: the smaller number—120 as opposed to 135— indicates the higher value. But golf scores, after all, are just as backward.)

47

So you decide to take your profits by trading your
13,500 yen for dollars. At 120 yen per dollar, that exchange
grosses you $112.50—a 12½ percent profit in three months.
Not bad at all. And, incidentally, not unrealistic. With the
right timing, you could have done about that well in the
fall of 1988. You can follow the fortunes of the yen from
1986 to 1988 in figure 3–1. Reading a yen/dollar chart is
a little tricky. You have to know that the numbers on the
left represent the dollar value of 10,000 yen. For example,
80 indicates that 10,000 yen equal $80 at the current ex-
change rate. To get the value of 1 yen in dollars, you have
to move the decimal four places to the left. That would
give you 0.0080 dollars per yen, which is .80 cents, or 8/10
of one penny. Yen play a large role in the world, but are
very small units of currency. For mathematical purposes,
it's easier to think of them in groups of 10,000 than one
at a time.

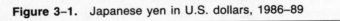

Figure 3–1. Japanese yen in U.S. dollars, 1986–89

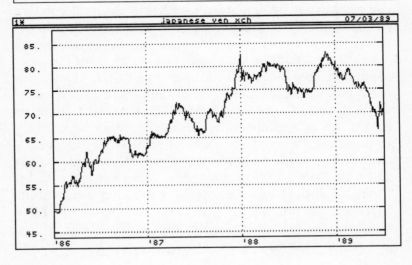

So, how do you get from 10,000 yen equals 80 dollars to the number of yen per dollar? Divide 10,000 by 80:

$$\frac{10,000}{80} = 125$$

One dollar, then, is the equivalent of 125 yen. You will most often see the exchange rate given in this form, since it's easier to work with whole numbers such as 125 than with decimals such as 0.0080. At any rate, your bank account will contain a vast quantity of yen in comparison with the number of dollars you exchange for the initial deposit.

Holding yen at the bank isn't the only way to speculate on the fluctuations of the yen/dollar exchange rate. Money is more than a medium of exchange; it is a commodity like pork bellies or coffee beans. So you can buy and sell futures contracts on most of the world's major currencies, just as you can for other commodities.

When you buy a yen futures contract, you agree to exchange a certain amount in dollars for a certain amount in yen on some specified date. If the yen appreciates, then you win—because the yen you buy have increased in purchasing power, while the dollars you give up have shrunk in purchasing power. You can speculate in currency options—which are rather like futures, only they don't obligate the owner of the contract to do anything. Instead, they confer on the purchaser the option to exchange dollars for yen or not to do so, depending on which makes more sense at the specified date.

Once again, why not just speculate in the currencies? Because you want the equity value of the investment as well as the currency value. The shares you buy represent ownership in a company, a stake in a nation's economy, and a chance to accumulate wealth over the long term. Currency speculation is, well, speculative. It involves careful timing and intensive study to profit from short-term shifts in the value of one currency against another.

Stocks can be played that way, too, of course—but in chapter 6 we will urge you to look on your foreign stock investments as long-term growth vehicles rather than short-term speculative instruments. We emphatically do not believe that foreign equities belong in the short-term, speculative part of your portfolio.

If you buy Matsushita Electric Corporation (Matsushita) or Mitsubishi or Hitachi Magnetics Corporation (Hitachi), for example, you're investing in a number of factors—their products, management, and balance-sheet numbers; the economic vision and policies of Japan's leadership; alterations in the yen/dollar exchange rate. Over the long term, the changing dollar value of the yen is probably not going to be the decisive factor in the success of your investment. But it is one factor.

So we devote the rest of this chapter to exchange-rate basics, paying special attention to the two reasons an equity investor cares about currency—to be sure you're buying and selling at the right price; to follow the changing value of your stocks.

The Basics of Currency Exchange

Before you buy a Japanese security, you buy the yen to purchase the security. At that point you find out what the stock is worth in dollars per share. Then you can make some comparisons with U.S. securities.

You go through a similar process as a tourist in Japan when you buy, say, a camera. The store clerk quotes you a price in yen, and you begin the puzzling and slightly threatening business of figuring how many of your dollars and pennies you need to purchase the item. Once you do that, you can compare the price to what you'd pay back home to buy the camera. Then you figure in any other expenses, such as customs duty, and decide whether or not the camera is a good deal.

And so it goes with stocks. You start by converting the foreign price if you want to do comparison shopping with U.S. securities. Then of course you go on to calculate any costs besides the price—commissions if you're using a foreign broker, taxes, fees, withholding on dividends, and so forth. If you like the rest of the calculations, you buy.

Back to the camera. Once you've bought the camera, you probably can stop worrying about the dollar value of yen. You buy a camera to take pictures, not to hold for appreciation. Its value to you is recorded in pictures and prints, not in its resale price on the second-hand camera market. Unless you're involved in some sort of gray-market camera scheme.

While you hold a Japanese security, on the other hand, you care very much about its current value in the marketplace. The marketplace measures the security's value in yen. But after you purchase a stock, the rate of exchange between yen and dollar changes up or down. It's possible that you might sell the security for the same number of yen required to purchase it initially, but not be able to get as much of your currency in exchange for those yen. Or you might get more of your currency. The fluctuating exchange rate can work for you or against you.

The effects can be dramatic. In 1976, for example, 1 U.S. dollar was the equivalent of 300 yen in the currency-exchange market. That's about 0.0033 yen per dollar, or 33.3 on the yen/dollar chart we studied earlier. By the middle of 1986, the yen was up to 61 on the chart. And in 1988 it ranged in value from 73 to 82.5. A U.S. investor holding Japanese stocks in that 12-year period would have watched the growing dollar value of the yen with great glee. Every time the yen went up, the investor's stocks were worth more in U.S. dollars. Being invested in yen-denominated securities, assuming you didn't buy losers, was a nice way to hedge against inflation and the decline in purchasing power of the dollar.

Other Countries, Other Currencies

Now take a look at several other currency charts for 1986 to 1988 (figures 3–2 through 3–6). The basic story is simple: the French franc, the German mark, the Canadian dollar, and the Australian dollar all gained ground on the U.S. dollar. The mark that would buy less than half a dollar in early 1986 had, by early 1988, become the equivalent of about $.63. (Then it slipped a bit.) That steep uphill climb in late 1987 marks the post–Black Monday period, during which the U.S. dollar lost value at the same time the U.S. stock market was down. From 1985 to 1988, then, the mark grew 50 percent in value against the U.S. dollar.

Over in Mrs. Thatcher's domain, the British pound in early 1985 had slipped to about $1.35. (In more Imperial times, the pound was worth almost US$5.) By early 1988, the pound was back up to about $1.90—a gain of more than 40 percent and a bonus for U.S. investors who owned British stocks during those years.

In every case we've charted here—Japan, Germany, the United Kingdom, Canada, and Australia, U.S. investors could have capitalized on the appreciation of foreign currencies against the dollar—by trading the currency or stocks denominated in the currency. Whether or not they made money on appreciation in the stock's price, they profited from the change in currency values. Keeping track of gains and losses is one good reason for carefully watching the news about currencies when you hold foreign stocks.

But how does it work? Let's invent some relatively simple cases to see how currency exchange might have affected your foreign stocks during 1986 to 1988, when the dollar was in general decline. Let's consider the United Kingdom and Australia, and, for simplicity's sake, assume a level price for our stocks. So everything that transpires in our hypothetical account will be due to currency fluctuation.

52

Figure 3–2. French franc in U.S. dollars, 1986–89

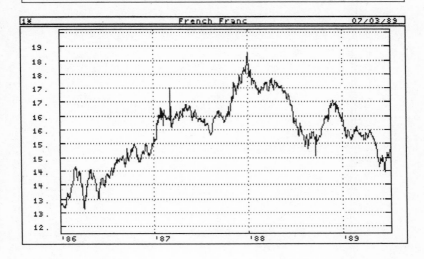

Figure 3–3. German mark in U.S. dollars, 1986–89

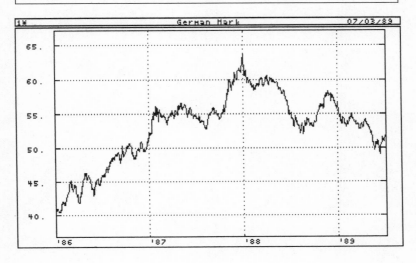

Figure 3-4. British pound in U.S. dollars, 1986–89

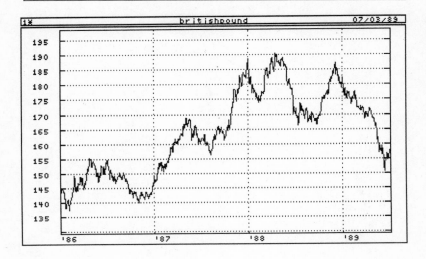

Figure 3-5. Canadian dollar in U.S. dollars, 1986–89

Figure 3–6. Australian dollar in U.S. dollars, 1986–89

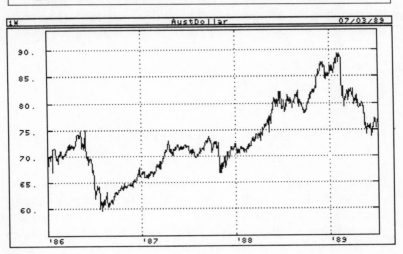

Since we need money to do this, we'll give ourselves US$10,000 to invest in each country when the dollar is still fairly strong—early 1985. Then we'll see what happens to our invested capital as the currency exchange rates vary and the stock prices remain constant.

First, the United Kingdom. Refer back to figure 3–4. In January of 1986, we invest $10,000 in British securities. At the time, the pound is trading at $1.40 (140 on the preceding chart). The stocks, of course, are quoted in pounds on the ISE in London. So we need to figure out, first of all, how many pounds we can get with our $10,000. We know that £1 is equal to $1.40, and we can write that as an equation:

$$\$1.40 = £1$$

But what we want to know is the value of 1 dollar, so we divide 1.40 by 1.40 to get $1 on the left side of the equation.

Then, to keep the equation in balance, we divide the other side by 1.40. Dividing 1 by 1.40 gives us .71429. Each dollar is worth .71429 pounds. The arithmetic looks like this:

$$\$1.40 = £1$$

$$\frac{\$1.40}{1.40} = \frac{£1}{1.40}$$

$$\$1 = £.71429$$

$$\text{Exchange rate} = .71429 \text{ pounds/dollar}$$

$$\$10,000 = £7,143$$

Because $10,000 is an easy number to work with, the conversion from dollars to pounds looks pretty straightforward. That won't always be the case. For tougher conversions, we'll use a common-sense, almost nonmathematical method for conversion, and we'll provide a good deal of practice.

Consider again the conversion of $10,000 into £7,143 when the exchange ratio is 1.40 pounds to the dollar. What's the shortest route from $10,000 to £7,143? Can we cut out the intermediate step of changing the ratio of dollars per pound (1.40) into pounds per dollar (.7143)? Sure. Whenever you have one currency to convert to another, all you need to know is the value of one currency and one version of the exchange rate. The only decision you have to make is whether to multiply or divide. The simplest way to make the choice is to determine whether you want to end up with a larger or smaller number.

So here's how that applies to the exchange of $10,000 into currency suitable for buying stocks in the United Kingdom. We have $10,000. We have the ratio: 1 pound is equivalent to $1.40. How do we decide whether to multiply or divide? Just ask whether you want a bigger or smaller number. That is, will our number of pounds be smaller or larger than our number of dollars (10,000)? It will be smaller.

One dollar is less than one pound, O.K.? So to make 10,000 smaller, do we multiply or divide by 1.40? Multiplying $10,000 by 1.40 will yield a larger number, since we would be multiplying by more than 1. Multiplying $10,000 by 1.40 would be a mistake. (We would wind up with 14,000 pounds). So we divide $10,000 by 1.40 dollars per pound and we come up with £7,143 (rounded off).

All you ever have to worry about in currency exchange, then, is whether you want to get a bigger or smaller number, and whether or not the exchange rate is more or less than 1. If the rate is more than 1, you multiply to get a larger number, divide to get a smaller number. If the rate is less than 1, you multiply to get a smaller number, divide to get a larger number.

So we have £7,143 to spend on British securities. We listen to our broker's advice, do our own research, and decide how to allocate that money. Then we hold our stock until September of 1988, at which point our U.K. investment is still worth exactly £7,143. If we decide we've grown tired of this stodgy collection of stocks and sell them, how will we come out?

First, the sale. That gives a gross return of £7,143. (Since we're making the rules here, we won't pay any commissions or taxes.) We call our banker or broker, or look in the paper, and discover that the pound is currently worth about $1.72. Has the pound grown stronger or weaker since 1985? Substantially stronger. When we opened our position, the pound would only buy $1.40. So we will have made some money in dollars, even though the price of the stocks in pounds stayed the same. How much money?

We have £7,143. One pound is equal to $1.72. So we'll have a larger number of dollars after exchanging them for pounds. Do we multiply 7,143 by 1.72, or do we divide? To get a larger number, we multiply.

$$£7,143 \times \$1.72/pound = \$12,285.96$$

The movement of the two currencies was good to us. We gained more than 25 percent on a stock that didn't change in price. The corporate stock side of our transaction was a bust; the currency side pulled us through. While we held our British investments, the pound strengthened, the dollar weakened, and we made money on securities that seemed dead in the water. We can be grateful, on the sale of our position, to the Thatcher government for pursuing policies that helped us make a profit. Or we can take rueful pleasure in knowing that our overseas investment provided something of a hedge against a decline in the value of our home currency.

Now let's see how we made out with the $10,000 we put into Australian stock. (Refer back to figure 3-6.)

The exchange situation between the United States and Australia is the reverse of the U.S.-U.K. relationship: One U.S. dollar is worth more than one Australian dollar, whereas one U.S. dollar is worth less than one pound. In early 1986, when we want to convert our U.S. dollars into Australian currency, the rate is about .70 U.S. dollars per one Australian dollar.

First question: will our US$10,000 convert to a greater or smaller number of Aussie dollars?

A greater number. Why? The Australian dollars are smaller. It takes more of them, figuratively speaking, to fill up the same space occupied by a given number of U.S. dollars.

So, do we multiply or divide by the exchange rate? Since .70 is less than one, multiplying it times $10,000 would yield an answer smaller than $10,000 — $7,000, to be precise. And we need more Aussie dollars than that to purchase stock worth $10,000 in U.S. currency.

So we divide:

$$\frac{US\$10,000}{.70} = Aus\$14,286$$

Our $10,000 buys us $14,286 worth of Australian securities. Which, when we sell them in September 1988, are still worth $14,286 (rounded off).

The Australian dollars we receive for the securities, however, are no longer worth only $.70 in U.S. currency. Like the British pound, Australia's dollar has grown in value compared to the U.S. dollar. In late 1988, an Australian dollar can be exchanged for $.85 in U.S. currency. Again, our stocks have gone neither up nor down in price, but we've made money on the currency side of the investment.

How much have we made? We know the Australian dollars received for our stock will exchange for a smaller number of U.S. dollars. So we multiply by .85—because multiplying $14,286 by a number less than one (.85) will give us a number less than $14,286.

$$Aus\$14,286 \times .85 = US\$12,143$$

And that's enough of hypothetical examples. Next we'll take a look at a real-world position. The important point of working the two preceding examples is to experience a way of thinking. You can follow many of your foreign stocks simply by calling your broker occasionally for a quote in U.S. dollars. By all means, let the broker do the calculations if you wish. But you must acquire the basic mode of thought necessary to follow an investment denominated in another currency.

You're an international investor now, so you need to be able to think clearly about the part that currency fluctuation plays in your net worth. If you invest in a country whose currency is strengthening in relationship to your own currency, you can realize a substantial gain—even on stocks that don't appreciate a great deal. Conversely, if you invest in a country with a weakening currency, you can lose money on a security that doesn't decline in price.

You also need to be able to convert one currency into

another. We've practiced that some, we'll practice it more later. When doing conversions, remember to watch for the relative size: are you going from a smaller to a larger number of units (from US$1 to 135 yen, for example)? Or are you converting a larger number of units into a smaller number (Aus$1 into US$.85, for example)? Keeping in mind the relative sizes of currencies helps you check your arithmetic. Any conversion into yen that yields a small number, for instance, is bound to be wrong!

Case Studies

Now for the real world, in which exchange rates and stock prices fluctuate at the same time. We'll put U.S. dollars into Matsushita, and follow the fate of our invested capital from early August of 1987 through Black Monday and on into late April of 1988. To make this a story with a happy ending, let's buy during the week of August 3, 1987, with Matsushita trading at around 2600 yen/share, and chart the progress of our investment until April 26, 1988, when the stock has risen from the black hole after Black Monday to a respectable price of 2800 yen/share. The following chart of the Japanese market during those eight months shows just what you would expect: a wild swing downward in late 1987 followed by a fairly strong recovery. Through all those months, Matsushita followed the market.

This isn't, however, the whole story for our investment. During those months, the yen, as the next chart reveals, travels a rather bumpy course. Overall, it goes up from August 1987 to April 1988. But it isn't a simple one-way trip.

During the week of August 3, when Matsushita is trading at about 2600 yen, the yen is worth about $.0067 – 67 on the chart. That means you need about 150 yen to purchase 1 U.S. dollar (1 divided by .0067 is 149 and a fraction). If we take our yen to the bank and place them on the

Figure 3–7. The Nikkei Index, Aug. 1987–Oct. 1988

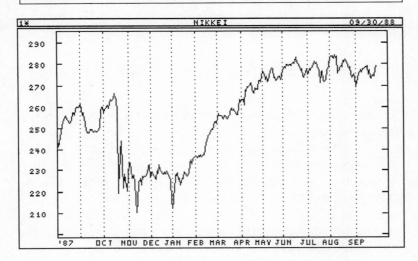

Figure 3–8. Japanese yen in U.S. dollars, Jan. 1987– Nov. 1988

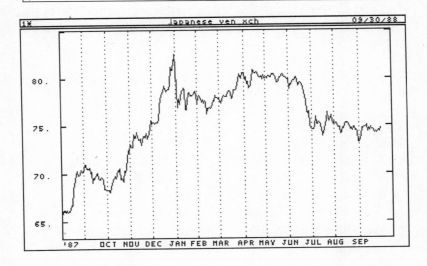

teller's counter in neat stacks of 150 each, we will receive 1 U.S. dollar for each stack of 150 yen. Arithmetically, that's just how we calculate the price per share of Matsushita in dollars: divide 2600 yen by 150.

$$\frac{2600 \text{ yen}}{150} = \$17.33/\text{share}$$

Our Matsushita purchase runs us $17.33 a share. After we buy the stock, two months pass and it's the week of October 5. All seems reasonably right with the world, and Matsushita has risen on the Tokyo Stock Exchange to a value of 2800 yen. That's an increase of about 7.7 percent from its price of 2600 yen/share in early August. We have cause to rejoice in an annualized gain approaching 50 percent.

Moreover, during the same two months, the yen has been gaining strength against the dollar—as you can tell by the rapidly rising line on the yen-dollar exchange chart. By early October, the yen is up to about 69 ($.0069), which is about 145 yen per dollar. The yen is growing stronger. Or the dollar is getting weaker; one dollar will now get you 145 yen instead of 150—the rate when we opened the position in August. Not only is our stock worth more, but so is the currency in which it is denominated. This will magnify our gains.

$$\frac{2800}{145} = \text{US\$19.31}$$

This increase from $17.33 to $19.31 represents an 11.43 percent appreciation in the dollar value of our position—a substantial improvement on the 7.7 percent rise in the price of the stock in yen.

If we were really prescient, we would sell our position soon, because we're very close to the stock's peak price. But in fact we're in Matsushita for the long term and we're not trading on what we think is going to happen in the next few weeks or months.

So we hang onto Matsushita and endure the terrors of October 19. On that date, we do not panic and sell. Instead, we hold our position. In the early part of November, things look very bleak. During the week of the 16th, the price of Matsushita drops through 1900 for the second time since the beginning of the month. But the yen keeps gaining on the dollar. It's up to 73 now, or about 136 yen to the dollar. And this cushions our fall a bit. The dollar price of Matsushita in the middle of November is about $13.97:

$$\frac{1900}{136} = \$13.97$$

The drop from about 2800 yen per share to 1900 yen per share (and worse) is a calamitous 32 percent. The yen has gained a little, though, so the decline in the dollar value of our position, from $19.31 to $13.97, isn't quite so horrendous. Still, that's a loss of about 28 percent. Just the same, the success of our currency strategy provides some compensation for the bad luck we're having with the stock itself. This is no way to get rich, to be sure, but we're happy for whatever small consolation is available while we ride out the storm following Black Monday. In fact, if we're very smart investors, and unusually brave, we'll increase the size of our position in Matsushita this week.

We celebrate the new year and resolve to hang onto our Japanese equities. January is a hard month for us, because the yen drops sharply against the dollar. But spring comes, and we find that Matsushita has returned to 2600 yen/share by the week of March 25, 1988—the price we paid for it in August the previous year. We've come full circle with our stock position. The yen, meanwhile, peaked in early January at 82.5—about 121 yen/dollar, faltered briefly and fell below 74, then rose again to 80.5, or about 124 yen to the dollar. In U.S. currency, then, our position is worth almost $21 per share:

$$\frac{2600}{124} = \$20.96$$

Back in August of 1987, when Matsushita was trading at 2600 yen, each share was worth only $17.33 — because it took 150 yen to buy a dollar. Now we can exchange a mere 124 yen for a U.S. dollar: the continuing appreciation of the yen, along with Matsushita's recovery, keeps putting dollars in our pocket.

In late April, the week of the 25th, the yen has slipped very slightly, to 125 per dollar, but Matsushita has risen again to 2800 yen per share. We can feel vindicated for not selling in early October: the price has recovered fully to its precrash level. Not only that, but the progressive strengthening of the yen has continued to increase the dollar value of our position.

$$\frac{2800}{125} = \$22.40/\text{share}$$

Compared to the value of the stock when we bought it for $17.33 a share, this represents an appreciation of 29 percent in our position in about eight months. It was an exciting — and scary — two-thirds of a year; but our reward for hanging on is an annualized gain of better than 45 percent in the dollar value of our stock. We'll never say the foreign markets are boring.

Here's a summary chart, showing yen and dollar prices of Matsushita, along with percentage gains in the value of the position, for selected dates between August 3, 1987 and April 25, 1988:

Table 3–1.   A Wild Ride with Matsushita

Week Of	Price/Share	% Change
8/3/87	2600 yen	NA
	$17.33	NA
10/5/87	2800 yen	+ 7.69
	$19.31	+ 11.43
11/16/87	1900 yen	– 32.14
	$13.97	– 27.65
12/7/87	2100 yen	+ 10.53
	$15.79	+ 13.03
2/8/88	2200 yen	+ 4.76
	$17.05	+ 7.98
3/28/88	2600 yen	+ 18.18
	$20.96	+ 22.93
4/25/88	2800 yen	+ 7.69
	$22.40	+ 6.87

Calculating Exchange Rates

Window shopping, as we said in chapter 1, has its place in global investment. Just opening a newspaper or magazine to the section on foreign exchange and foreign currencies puts one in touch with the wider world. The names of the world's great corporations—the banks, the automotive companies, the electronics corporations, globe-spanning airlines—are more and more part of our everyday news. Deutsche Bank, Honda Motors Company (Honda), British Airways, Deutsche Lufthansa (Lufthansa): they speak to us of great fortunes, great adventures, perhaps of great risks. They are emblems of our time, symbolizing not only growth and change, but also tradition and stability. Nor can one read a column of exchange rates without seeing visions of foreign lands, marketplaces, bazaars where goods and money circulate: dollars, pounds, marks, francs, pesos, guilders, riyals, yen, lira, and bolivars, each conjuring its own scenes and sounds and smells.

In this section we'll establish our own small market-place, and practice purchasing and selling stocks from selected countries, exchanging our currencies as necessary.

We'll use the exchange rates and stock prices current on Tuesday, September 6, 1988, a day on which nothing of great note happened. The U.S. dollar held steady against the Canadian dollar, and continued its slide against the yen, the pound, the mark, and other European currencies. Business as usual.

From the more than four dozen currencies routinely covered in the financial news, Table 3–2 provides a selected list of exchange rates on that Tuesday. In the middle column is the U.S. equivalent of each country's currency. The right-hand column converts one unit of each country's currency into U.S. dollars.[1] Take, for example, the first entry, the Australian dollar. The middle column tells us that US$0.8050 is equivalent to $1 of Australian currency. The right-hand column tells us that Aus$1.2422 will get you $1 in U.S. currency.

In terms of securities, that means that a stock listed for $10 a share (Australian dollars) on the exchange in Sydney is worth US$8.05. It also tells us that $10 of U.S. currency, since it can be exchanged for about $12.42 Australian, will buy 1.24 shares of the $10 stock.

More of that later.

One of the confusing things about exchange rates is that they can be quoted from either side of the currency transaction. The exchange rate between pounds and U.S. dollars, for example, can be quoted either as 1.70 (dollars per pound) or .58 (pounds per dollar). One can get a little dizzy from the directional changes. Nor does it help that the units of global currency are so vastly disproportionate in size. It boggles the American mind to discover that one needs almost 135 yen, more than 721 Korean won, or 1606 Turkish lira to equal $1. And these disparities further complicate matters because they require one to work with exchange

Table 3–2. Exchange Rates on September 6, 1988

Country	U.S. Dollars per Currency Unit	Currency Units per U.S. Dollar
Australia (dollar)	0.8050	1.2422
Brazil (cruzado)	0.003315	301.70
United Kingdom (pound)	1.7030	0.5872
Canada (dollar)	0.8091	1.2360
China (yuan)	0.2693	3.7127
France (franc)	0.1594	6.2725
Japan (yen)	0.007413	134.90
Saudi Arabia (riyal)	0.2667	3.750
South Korea (won)	0.001386	721.30
Switzerland (franc)	0.6441	1.5525
Turkey (lira)	0.000623	1606.00
West Germany (mark)	0.5427	1.8425

ratios such as .001386 (for the won) and .000623 (for the Turkish lira).

Nevertheless, each calculation boils down to two numbers that you either multiply or divide. In the age of inexpensive calculators, this is really not too daunting, once you get over the dizziness.

So let's do a few sample calculations, converting currencies back and forth to see what some typical stock transactions would cost—or yield—on Tuesday, September 6.

Let's say you've decided to sell 500 shares of Sony and reinvest the proceeds in Pearson Ltd. (Pearson), a diversified British holding company, and in the German airline company, Lufthansa (which is quoted in marks).

These are the relevant stock prices on September 6:

Sony: 6,770 yen per share
Pearson: 719 pence per share
Lufthansa: 142 marks per share

First, calculate the yen value of 500 shares of Sony:

500 Sony at 6,770 yen per share = 3,385,000 yen

How many U.S. dollars will we get for our yen when we sell 500 shares of Sony? We have a choice of two versions of the exchange rate: 0.007413 (dollars per yen) or 134.90 (yen per dollar). We can use either one. Let's take the one in the middle column, 0.007413.

What do we do with this tiny decimal—multiply it by 3,385,000 or divide it into that amount?

The answer depends on whether you want a number smaller or larger than 3,385,000. And that's easy to determine in this case. Since it takes a shoeboxful of yen to equal a dollar, we want to reduce this very large number to a much smaller one. Working with a tiny decimal fraction like 0.007413, we do that by multiplication.

Since this is practice, take out your calculator. Punch in 3,385,000, then hit the multiplication sign. Next punch in 0.007413. When you push the equals (=) button, you should get an answer of 25,093.00:

3,385,000 yen × .007413 dollars/yen = 25,093.00 dollars

When you take your 3,385,000 yen to the bank, therefore, you can exchange them for $25,093.00.

Just for fun, see what happens when you use the other conversion factor, 134.90 yen per dollar. Since this is a factor much larger than one, you need to divide it into the number of yen to yield a smaller number of dollars. So punch up 3,385,000 on your calculator, hit the division sign, put in 134.90, and hit the equals sign, and look for the same answer you received using the dollars-per-yen rate:

$$\frac{3,385,000 \text{ yen}}{134.90 \text{ yen/dollar}} = \$25,092.66$$

Well, close enough. When you're working with so many decimal places, things tend toward the approximate. Your banker's computer will be more exact.

At any rate, you now have $25,000 and change to reinvest in Pearson and Lufthansa.

How many shares of each can you get?

First you decide to convert the per-share prices of each stock into U.S. dollars to see how they compare. Pearson is trading at 719 pence, or £7.19 per share. One pound currently costs $1.7030. Though the pound has shrunk a bit since its imperial days, it's still a larger unit of exchange than the dollar. When you convert your U.S. currency into pounds, therefore, you will need a larger number of dollars than the number of pounds you hope to receive. Multiplying by 1.7030 dollars per pound will give you that large number:

7.19 pounds × 1.7030 dollars/pound = 12.2446 dollars

Another simplified way to approach conversions is to set up the equation with currency names instead of numbers, like this:

$$\text{pounds} \times \frac{\text{dollars}}{\text{pounds}} = \text{dollars}$$

The pounds cancel out, leaving you with dollars equal to dollars. That lets you know that you've put the quantities in the proper order. If you had put the pounds-per-dollar figure into the equation in place of dollars-per-pound, you would have nothing to cancel and the left side would clearly not equal the right.

What about the dollar price of Lufthansa? On the Frankfurt exchange, the stock is trading at 142 marks/share. The mark is equivalent to 0.5427 dollars. (Or, the other way around, each of your dollars will purchase 1.8425 marks.) We'll multiply the dollars/mark amount, which is less than one, by the number of marks per share:

$$142 \text{ marks} \times .5427 \frac{\text{dollars}}{\text{mark}} = 77.0634 \text{ dollars}$$

From our calculations, we learn that Lufthansa is a much more expensive stock than Pearson.

Pearson: $12.24/share ($1,224 per 100 shares)
Lufthansa: $77.06/share ($7,706 per 100 shares)

So you might decide to purchase 200 shares of Lufthansa for just over $15,000, and spend the remaining $10,000 (speaking approximately) to pick up 800 shares of Pearson. You've actually spent a total of $25,204 dollars and exceeded your $25,093 budget a bit. So it goes.

What if you're considering the sale of a Japanese stock and subsequent purchase of a British or German stock, and you don't want to convert all the amounts into dollars first? The exchange rate for yen against marks and pounds will be readily available. In another country, however, you may have to make the conversions in terms of a third currency.

Here's an example. Let's say you own a great many shares of Honda, and would like to diversify within the auto industry by acquiring stock in Jaguar, Volkswagen Inc. (Volkswagen) and Peugeot Motors Inc. (Peugeot). First, the prices:

Honda: 2,090 yen per share
Jaguar: £2.46 per share
Volkswagen: 248.5 marks per share
Peugeot: 1,140 francs per share

The exchange rates for each currency, in U.S. dollars, are as follows:

Yen: 134.90 per dollar
Pound: 0.5872 per dollar
Mark: 1.8425 per dollar
Fr. franc: 6.2725 per dollar

You can use the U.S. exchange rates to make your own conversion tables. For example, the number of yen per British pound is the yen's exchange rate over (divided by) the pound's exchange rate:

$$\frac{134.90 \text{ yen/\sout{dollar}}}{0.5872 \text{ pound/\sout{dollar}}} = 229.7343$$

As before, you can make verbal sense out of this calculation by letting the dollars cancel out. You wind up with a calculation that literally tells you the number of yen per pound (yen/pound). And since the pound is a larger unit of exchange than the dollar, it makes intuitive sense that a pound would equal more yen (at 229+ yen per pound) than does a dollar (at 134+ yen per dollar).

Now, what is the price of Jaguar in yen?

Jaguar is £2.46 per share
One pound is equal to 229.7343 yen
Therefore, Jaguar is 2.46 × 229.7343 yen per share

£2.46 × 229.7343 yen/pound = 565.1464 yen/share
And, 100 shares of Jaguar is 56,514.64 yen

As we go through the same type of calculation to convert the prices of Volkswagen and Peugeot into yen, use your calculator to do each step yourself for practice. First, do the currency conversions.

Mark: 1.8425 per dollar
Yen: 134.9000 per dollar

From this information, is it possible to find the exchange rate for marks and yen? Yes. Since you know the relationship of both to a third currency (U.S. dollars) you can calculate their relationship to one another. To do so, would you multiply, divide, add, or subtract?

Divide. You are constructing an exchange ratio express-
ing the number of yen per mark. A ratio is a fraction, which
is simply a division problem. For example, the fraction 1/2
is 1 divided by 2.

Which number goes on top: marks per dollar, or yen
per dollar?

Yen per dollar. Why? Because yen/dollar over marks/
dollar gives you the number of yen per mark:

$$\frac{\text{yen/\sout{dollar}}}{\text{marks/\sout{dollar}}}$$

What, then, is the exchange ratio of yen to marks?

$$\frac{134.90 \text{ yen/dollar}}{1.8425 \text{ marks/dollar}} = 73.2157 \text{ yen/mark}$$

Each mark is equivalent to 73.2157 yen. Looking back at
our stock chart, we see Volkswagen trading at 248.5 marks
per share. We know that the price per share in yen will
be substantially higher, since it takes over 73 yen to equal
1 mark. So the calculation is simple multiplication:

$$248.5 \text{ marks/share} \times 73.2157 \text{ yen/mark} =$$
$$18{,}194.101 \text{ yen/share}$$

Now we convert francs to yen to determine a price for
Peugeot in yen/share. This time we'll leave out the steps
and go straight to the solution.

We know we want a ratio of yen to francs, which is the
fraction with yen per dollars on top and francs per dollar
below.

$$\frac{\text{yen/dollar}}{\text{francs/dollar}} = \frac{134.9000}{6.2725} = 21.5066$$

Each franc, then, is equivalent to 21.5066 yen. And the price of Peugeot in yen?

> Peugeot is trading at 1,140 francs per share.
> Each franc is worth 21.5066 yen.
> Each share of Peugeot costs 1,140 × 21.5066 yen.
> Peugeot: 24,517.524 yen per share.

Here's the revised currency exchange table:

> One pound: 229.7343 yen
> One mark: 73.2157 yen
> One franc: 21.5066 yen

And here's the revised stock chart:

> Jaguar: 565.15 yen/share
> Volkswagen: 18,194.10 yen/share
> Peugeot: 24,517.52 yen/share

All that remains for the investor is to make choices. If you sell, say, 5,000 shares of Honda at 2,090 yen per share, you'll have 10,450,000 yen to work with. You have many stocks and currencies to choose from. Begin slowly and, over the long term, you'll find your comfort zone. Most of all, enjoy.

Conclusion to Part One

In our tour of the global marketplace, we've covered the basics of what's available in foreign stocks—mutual funds, closed-end funds, ADRs, and foreign shares purchased through a domestic or foreign broker. And we've done the intellectual background work required before making investment decisions. The time has come to get practical, and chapter 4 gets right down to the basic questions investors have about owning foreign stocks. You want to find the right type of broker for your needs and ask the right questions—the ones that will nail down the information you need to be sure you get what you pay for. After that, we'll look at pitfalls to avoid (chapter 5), fundamental and technical analysis of foreign stocks (chapters 6 and 7), and the workings of other markets (chapter 8).

Endnotes

1. All information on currency rates and stock prices cited in the following examples is taken from *The Wall Street Journal*, September 7, 1988, p. 34.

PART II

GLOBAL STRATEGIES

CHAPTER 4

How to Trade Foreign Stocks

You're excited about a foreign stock. You're bullish on the country, comfortable with the industry, convinced the company is well managed and poised to prosper. To assess the health of the currency, you've consulted *Barron's, Investor's Daily,* or other sources. If this were a domestic company, you'd call your broker and buy. But it's not a domestic company, and your mind fills up with practical questions about what to do next:

> Can I just call up my usual broker?
> Can I pay with a check in U.S. dollars or do I have to pay in a foreign currency?
> Do I buy in 100-share lots?
> Do I pay now or later?

You're asking, in other words, "How do I buy that?" In this chapter, we will answer that—and other practical questions. Because other questions probably will occur to you, questions about what happens after the purchase:

Do I receive a written confirmation?
Who holds the stock certificates?
Are certificates available?
Will the dividends, proxies, and annual reports arrive on time?
What about taxes?

But most of all, and first of all: How do I buy that?

It all depends—those three vexing words. You may find yourself going through your usual broker, looking for a new broker-dealer or banker, going to an overseas broker, or not using a broker at all. But whichever option is appropriate, the process is just a variation on the usual procedure you use when investing. You have an investment objective; reaching it will involve taking a certain number of steps; you take them one at a time; and pretty soon you've reached your goal. We'll tackle the various ways of buying foreign stocks in ascending order of complexity.

ADRs and U.S.-Based Investment Companies

In chapter 2 we discussed the hundreds of ADRs and dozens of closed- and open-end investment companies available for the investor who wants to get involved in domestically traded foreign equities.

All those securities are available to the U.S. investor in the normal ways. For ADRs and closed-end funds, you simply call a broker and place your order. Generally, you'll have the broker-dealer hold your securities rather than send you the certificates. Dividend checks, if there are any, will come to the broker-dealer and be sent along to you or deposited as you instruct. You'll receive reports from the company and statements from your broker.

If you choose a mutual fund—an open-end investment company—you might decide to buy directly from the fund rather than investing through a broker. That can usually be done by phone; just call the fund's 800 number. Or you can invest through the mail, taking a risk on price changes that occur while the paperwork is in process. The fund will send you confirmations and account statements along with their annual reports and, no doubt, their advertising.

At the end of the tax year, the fund or company you've invested in will send you a form with an accounting of all your dividends and capital gains, information you need for computing your taxes.

So much for relatively familiar ways to invest. What happens if you're enamored of a truly foreign security, one that isn't registered with the SEC, isn't part of a domestic investment company portfolio, isn't quoted in the domestic press, and isn't listed on an exchange or traded OTC?

The Truly Foreign Investment

It's always high noon on somebody's stock exchange. If not on Wall Street, then in London, Paris, and Amsterdam. If not in Western Europe, then in Tel Aviv or São Paulo, in Singapore or Tokyo. Any time of the day or night that you get a bright investment idea, someone, somewhere, is awake and taking orders.

But the rules differ from place to place—and from time to time. Just because someone is ready to do business with you doesn't mean that person will do business your way. Each country has, in addition to its own language, its own view of foreign investors, its own trading vocabulary, its particular schedule and method for settling trades, and so on. More on the varieties of investment experience shortly.

First, let's look at some things that stay the same wherever you trade—the three elements of securities ownership:

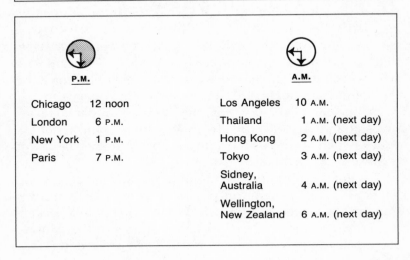

Figure 4–1. World Time Zones

P.M.		A.M.	
Chicago	12 noon	Los Angeles	10 A.M.
London	6 P.M.	Thailand	1 A.M. (next day)
New York	1 P.M.	Hong Kong	2 A.M. (next day)
Paris	7 P.M.	Tokyo	3 A.M. (next day)
		Sidney, Australia	4 A.M. (next day)
		Wellington, New Zealand	6 A.M. (next day)

1. Trading—when you enter an order for a security
2. Settling—when money and securities change hands
3. Holding—the ownership period, when, among other things, you may receive dividends and pay taxes

These three aspects of stock ownership are universal. But they don't happen quite the same in every country. And the variations on each can be quite significant—particularly during the holding period, when you make or lose your money.

Since there are so many exchanges, so many rules, and so much room for the rules to change, there's no point trying to describe every country's regulations here. As a wise investor, you should be ready to ask questions of the broker or banker you deal with, and to make no assumptions. At this point, your job is to learn the questions, not the answers. We'll go through each of the three parts of ownership, then we'll provide a script for talking to brokers about foreign stocks.

Variations That Affect Trading and Settlement

Not all exchanges permit the same types of orders. Margin buying and short selling, for instance, are not allowed in some countries. Round-lot sizes, too, vary from 1,000 shares for low-priced stock in Japan to 1 share for high-priced stocks in Switzerland.

A more serious difficulty arises in countries that restrict the flow of currency across the border. Thailand and Italy, for example, both maintain restrictions on the passage of currency out of the country. One can hardly help sympathizing with the Italians. You might buy stock in such a country—importing dollars into their economy in the process. But when you sell the stock, your currency may have to stay where it is. Living, as they do, next door to Switzerland, Italians are understandably concerned that their currency might vanish into bank vaults just across the border in, say, Lugano.

Settlement schedules, too, vary from country to country. Trades in the United States settle in five business days. Eurosecurities trading, mostly based in London, also features five-day settlement. On the ISE in London, however, certificates change hands for every trade, and the resulting paper chase stretches settlement out to a fortnight (At this writing, Londoners are bickering mightily about the proper changes to speed up the system.) On the Paris Bourse, trades settle in one month.

Most trading and settlement problems are mere nuisances. The investor who trades through a U.S. broker-dealer shouldn't even notice a difference in settlement schedule. Delays beyond five business days are usually the broker's concern, not the investor's. Sometimes, however, antiquated settlement systems break down, receipts and certificates accumulate unprocessed in a vault somewhere, and transactions aren't completed. At this writing, for example, investors in Spain sometimes wait as long as six months for trades to settle. (Don't feel too smug; this happened in the United States in 1968.) Such delays can be very unsettling for investors who want to take their profits or cut their losses, since a security that hasn't been settled sometimes can't be sold. Some money managers avoid countries with long or unpredictable settlement periods.

Variations Affecting Investors During the Holding Period

The potential for really serious problems is greatest during the holding period—especially when you've invested through a foreign broker. On the nuisance end of the spectrum, but worth noting, is the fact that some countries, Switzerland included, don't allow foreign investors to vote their shares. In others, such as Japan, the foreign investor has to pay for a domestic proxy to handle the voting. More seriously, vital information may not get to you in time to be useful. Dividends owed you may be late or lost. Tax liabilities you never expected can unpleasantly surprise you—and reduce your profits. Worst of all, your invested capital may disappear altogether when an uninsured broker-dealer goes bankrupt.

Before we get into the scary stuff, let's take a quick look at where you can find a broker to handle your foreign transactions.

Domestic Brokers

Do you have to go to a foreign broker? No. But you'll find many domestic broker-dealers unable or unwilling to handle foreign trades. You might logically expect help from such large international operations as Salomon Brothers, Inc. (Salomon) and Morgan Stanley and Company, Inc. (Morgan

Stanley). They certainly have all the necessary resources for foreign trading, but they are institutional investment houses, meaning they don't open accounts for individuals, not even for individuals as wealthy as large corporations or small nation-states. With their international trading rooms, offices around the world, research staffs specializing in foreign markets, and mechanized settlement procedures, they are set up to service institutions such as mutual funds, insurance companies, banks, and other broker-dealers.

On the other end of the scale, the smaller local and regional broker-dealers also will be unlikely to handle foreign trades for you. A firm with offices only in Denver or Minneapolis or Spokane simply can't compete in this market. Neither can a regional house such as Piper Jaffray & Hopwood Inc. or Baird Corporation, though they have offices in several states. A regional firm may accommodate an international trade, but its limited facilities will force it to find other firms to execute the transaction and hold the security.

So where can you go? The larger full-service and discount brokers in the United States will buy, sell, and hold foreign securities for you. You're sure to get help, for example, at full-service giants such as Merrill Lynch Pierce Fenner & Smith (Merrill Lynch), Dean Witter Reynolds Inc. (Dean Witter), and Shearson Lehman Hutton Inc. (Shearson). Among the discount houses, Charles Schwab and Co. Inc. (Schwab) handles foreign investing or try a foreign broker with U.S. branches, such as the Japanese giant, Nomura Securities Co. (Nomura).

Like Salomon and Morgan Stanley, these are global operations. Merrill Lynch has a seat on the Tokyo stock exchange. Dean Witter has had an office in Hong Kong for more than 20 years. Merrill Lynch and Shearson have offices in Switzerland. Schwab has offices in Europe and Hong Kong.

Unlike Salomon and Morgan Stanley, these are retail firms that do business with individuals—even individuals with modest amounts to invest. They will execute foreign trades for you, handle the settlement, and, if you like, hold the securities. That is, they will register the security in their own name rather than yours. It is then their responsibility to pass along to you all information and checks they receive as nominal stockholder.

With an international broker-dealer, you may be able to choose between trading through a U.S. and trading through a foreign branch. A domestic branch will report your transactions to you in U.S. dollars. If you use an overseas office—say, Merrill Lynch in London—transactions will be in the currency of your security, and your account will contain all the currencies that your portfolio represents. Exchange into dollars won't occur until you instruct the firm to make the conversion.

Perhaps your best place to enter orders for foreign securities is a money-center bank, such as Citicorp, Manufacturers Hanover Trust Company (Manufacturers Hanover) or Bankers Trust Company (Bankers Trust). Surprised? In the U.S., we're used to thinking of banks and broker-dealers as inherently separate institutions. That's because the Glass-Steagall act, a piece of Depression-era legislation, established an impermeable wall between commercial and investment banking. But it does not prohibit U.S. banks from owning non-U.S. broker-dealers (or U.S. brokers without investment banking functions). Moreover, these money-center banks have for decades had international connections. Security Pacific National Bank (Security Pacific), a truly global bank, maintains ties to securities markets in Australia, Japan, and the United Kingdom through its broker-dealer, Security Pacific Hoare Govett Ltd. (Hoare Govett). Citicorp has offices in 90 countries and owns the British investment firm, Citicorp Scrimgeour Vickers De Costa (Scrimgeour Vickers).

As banks and as brokers, these thoroughly international institutions have solid experience in handling individual accounts. Their trust departments hold securities for their clients. Their currency-exchange operations — open for 24-hour trading — keep them in touch with foreign markets. And they are familiar with foreign clearing firms, the varied dividend schedules of foreign securities, and the hazards of foreign taxation.

But such banks are still U.S.-based. If you want maximum familiarity with the rules and regulations of a particular foreign market, you will want an account with a broker or bank in that country.

Overseas Brokers

Not hampered by the Glass-Steagall prohibitions, or any other U.S. laws for that matter, foreign banks routinely combine commercial and investment banking functions. So if you happen to be overseas, you can drop into a bank or brokerage house to ask about the feasibility of opening an account. If you're at home, write the exchange for a list of appropriate broker-dealers, or consult the directories at your library. In some countries, you will find, regulations prohibit trading by nonresidents.

Making the first contact with a foreign broker is up to you. Only firms registered with the SEC are allowed to solicit business from U.S. citizens. The investment idea must be yours too. Similarly, you must initiate any trading in foreign securities that aren't SEC-registered. Even U.S. firms can't advertise or recommend unregistered stocks.

The advantage of using a foreign broker-dealer is the firm's familiarity with the market, with the security, and with all the applicable rules and risks. Obviously, the firm will be able to execute your trade and handle the settlement. A foreign broker is potentially a superior source of fact sheets and opinions — if someone remembers to send them to you. (It's unfortunately easy to overlook small accounts.) Of course, the information that does get to you may require translation before you can read it.

Commissions and fees may be higher if you use a foreign broker, although many countries are phasing out fixed commissions in favor of negotiable charges. In the United Kingdom, for example, commissions have been fully negotiable since the Big Bang, as the British called the restructuring of their stock market in 1986. Japan is moving toward variable commissions. Be sure to ask about trading costs before making a move. But in most cases, higher commissions shouldn't be a deterrent. For individual investors, buying foreign securities is inherently a long-range proposition. The information flow is simply too slow and too thin to allow the quick movement necessary for speculative trading. And when one expects to hold securities for several years, the anticipated growth will more than compensate for any marginal differences in acquisition costs.

Your foreign broker will also be able to hold your securities for you, unless you decide to take delivery of the certificates. Remember, some countries don't allow the certificates outside their borders. And there are disadvantages to taking possession of the certificates. For one thing, doing so reduces your flow of information from the broker — which might include notice of mergers and acquisitions. Nevertheless, there are also some advantages. If the security is in your name, you receive dividend checks directly. (Incidentally, they may come annually or semiannually rather than quarterly.) This means you can see how much tax is withheld from each payment. By contrast, a broker-dealer who holds your certificate may simply send a check for the net amount owed you, with no information about the amount withheld. You will then have to find out what the dividend should have been (not always an easy task with a foreign company) and calculate the tax. Knowing the amount of tax withheld is important, because you may take foreign taxes as a credit against your U.S. income tax. (See appendix 4, a copy of the U.S. tax forms one files to receive credit for foreign tax payments.)

Figure 4–2. Sample stock certificate

If you receive the certificates for safekeeping, you may sell the stock through any broker you choose. To do so, you sign the certificate or a separate document (procedures vary by country), have the signature guaranteed (in some cases), and handle the mailing yourself.

Broker Bankruptcy

And there's a bigger problem about leaving cash or securities with a foreign broker-dealer. Occasionally these firms, like their domestic counterparts, go bankrupt. Unlike U.S. firms, however, they may take your money down with them. If your U.S. broker-dealer goes under, you are insured for up to $500,000 per account, $100,000 of which can be cash or cash equivalents. This safety net is provided by the Securities Investor Protection Corporation (SIPC), a nonprofit corporation established by the Securities Investors Protection Act of 1970.

SIPC (the acronym is pronounced "Sip-ick") does not, of course, insure investors against losses due to market fluctuations or the bankruptcies of companies they invest in. When a U.S. broker-dealer approaches insolvency, the responsible exchange or other SRO (self-regulatory organization) tries to arrange a merger between the failing firm and another broker-dealer. If that isn't possible, SIPC seizes the firm's accounts and compensates each investor. If the firm's assets won't cover investors' losses (up to the $500,000/$100,000 limit), SIPC makes up the difference from its own funds.

No country other than the United States has investor protection approaching that provided by SIPC. In the United Kingdom, for example, a "compensation fund" is earmarked for stockholders who lose money because a broker defrauds them or goes bankrupt. As of 1989, however, this compensation is limited to £48,000—100 percent of the first £30,000 of loss plus 90 percent of the next £20,000. And that's nowhere near the $500,000 protection provided in the United States.

Is inadequate protection of investors' assets merely a theoretical risk? It is, to an extent, a manageable risk: one can search out the firms and countries with the best bankruptcy protection. Nevertheless, it is a real risk. Financial firms do go under. In 1987, in the aftermath of Black Monday, the losses of Hong Kong broker-dealers were so substantial that the government put together a $258 million rescue package to get the industry back on its feet. The guarantee corporation that was supposed to be ready to bail out investors had only $2.9 million. If you trade through a foreign broker, then, you add what might be called "broker risk" to the potential pitfalls of your investment. You may end up relying on the goodwill of someone else's government to rescue you after your broker goes under. As a precaution, you can have a certificate delivered to you or to a bank.

Other Risks

Next to the threat of waking up to find your broker-dealer has gone broke, other problems of working with overseas firms pale into mere nuisances. Most of these irritations arise from the difficulties of currency exchange. If you trade through a foreign broker, you can't send a personal check to cover your transactions. You have to go to a money-center bank in the nearest city and get a cashier's check or bank money order denominated in the appropriate foreign currency.

Similarly, dividends will come to you in foreign money which you will have to convert and deposit to your domestic account. If the dividend is a small check, the various fees and costs required to get it from the issuing company into your account may devour it completely. There is a way around that problem. In December of 1988, the FRB ruled that U.S. banks could accept foreign currency deposits, beginning December 31, 1989. You might, for example, be a U.S. investor who trades frequently in Australia and deposits the proceeds in a Citicorp account. In 1990, Citicorp will be able to accept Australian dollars in your account. And you can leave the money in that account, without converting it into U.S. dollars, until you need it. If you use it only for Australian trading, you never have to convert it. Moreover, such an account gives you the flexibility to transfer between currencies when the exchange rate is favorable.

Examples

Time to take a look at some names and numbers. If you've read to this point, you very likely have some favorite foreign stocks, companies not listed on an exchange or by NASDAQ. If this were a seminar, you could ask about them. Since it isn't, we'll pick three that might be of interest—not as recommendations, of course, but as examples. Browsing in the "Overseas Markets" section of *Barron's*, one might, for instance, become intrigued by Yamaha Motors Co., Ltd. (Yamaha) on the Tokyo exchange, Henkel Corporation (Henkel) on the Frankfurt exchange, and Ciba-Geigy Corporation (Ciba) on the Zurich exchange. Consumers around the world have become familiar with the Yamaha name on motorcycles (also on pianos and guitars, but Yamaha and Yamaha Motors trade separately). Henkel is synonymous with fine cutlery. Ciba-Geigy is often in the news for its pharmaceutical research.

Leafing through the other markets covered in *Barron's*, however, you would find no quotes for these stocks in U.S. dollars. So you would return to the overseas quotes, get out your calculator, and see what getting into these investments would cost you.

For each stock, we find two quotes, one under the "Last Week" column, the other under "Previous Week." So right away there is a difficulty: we have the price of the stock for the past two weeks, but not for today. This obviously has implications for following an investment in these companies. Table 4–1 shows what we would have read in *Barron's* for September 19, 1988. We are pleased to see that the momentum is upward in all cases. Or so it seems at first glance. But what do the numbers mean: 1,460 what? Yen, in Yamaha Motors' case. The quotes are in the currency of the firms' home countries. If we want to translate those numbers into dollar prices, we need to find some exchange rates.

So we look up the currency quotes, which, on the date in question appeared somewhat as they do in Table 4–2. Again, the information is not exactly up to date, but is based on closing prices for the past two weeks, so it corresponds to the data on the stock prices.

Table 4–1.

	Last week	Previous week
Yamaha Motors	1,460	1,380
Henkel	466.50	457
Ciba	3,230	3,205

Table 4–2.

Country	US$ Equivalent		Currency per US$	
	Fri.	Last Fri.	Fri.	Last Fri.
Japan (yen)	.007454	.00748	134.15	133.67
W. Germany (mark)	.5345	.5408	1.8710	1.8489
Switzerland (franc)	.6325	.6402	1.5810	1.5620

These two tables reprinted by permission of *Barron's* © Dow Jones & Company, Inc., September 19, 1988. All Rights Reserved Worldwide.

Which rate do we use for conversions? "US$ Equivalent" or "Currency per US$"? It doesn't matter, really. With one, we multiply; with the other, we divide. Now, which is which? Using the simplified procedure that we explained in the preceding chapter, we ask only whether we need to come up with a bigger or smaller number. In the case of Yamaha Motors, quoted at 1,460 yen per share, we want a smaller number. Since the dollar buys a great deal more than the yen, we don't need so many of them to buy a share of Yamaha stock. So we can either multiply by the tiny decimal (.007454) or divide by 134.15. The calculator could care less, but presuming a desire to avoid the numbingly small number, we'll take 134.15 (yen per dollar) and divide it into 1.460 (yen) to get about $10.88 per share.

$$\frac{1{,}460 \text{ yen/share}}{134.15 \text{ yen/dollar}} = \$10.88/\text{share}$$

At the end of the previous week, when Yamaha was trading at 1,380 and the dollar was worth 133.67 yen, a share of the stock would have cost us $10.32.

$$\frac{1{,}380 \text{ yen/share}}{133.67 \text{ yen/dollar}} = \$10.32/\text{share}$$

Now at least we have dollar-per share prices of recent vintage, even if we don't know what Yamaha Motors is doing today (Sept. 19, 1988). Before we ask what other information we might be missing for the Japanese stock, let's run the numbers for the German and Swiss securities— for the sake of comparison.

For Henkel, we have to convert 466.50 and 457 marks per share into dollars. Again, the foreign currency is smaller than the dollar, though not as much smaller as the yen. It takes about 1.8 marks to equal 1 U.S. dollar. After the conversion, therefore, we'll have a smaller number of dollars than the number of marks we had to begin with. We'll divide again. First, the preceding week:

$$\frac{466.50 \text{ marks/share}}{1.871 \text{ marks/dollar}} = \$249.33/\text{share}$$

Then, the week before that:

$$\frac{457 \text{ marks/share}}{1.8489 \text{ marks/dollar}} = \$247.17/\text{share}$$

The stock moved up two dollars a share, we're pleased to note. But the difference in per-share price between Henkel and Yamaha Motors might boggle the mind. Is Yamaha Motors so minor a player that its stock is worth barely 1/25th as much per share as Henkel's? As a matter of fact, Henkel is a larger company: it ranked number 137 on the Fortune 500 international list for 1987; Yamaha Motors was number 226. But that clearly doesn't explain the spread between per-share prices.

The real culprit here is the difference between Japanese and German market conventions. For a Japanese stock, Yamaha is not priced low at all. Nor, for a German stock, is Henkel priced especially high. On the Japanese exchanges, per-share prices tend to be so low that round lots are typically 1,000 shares. ADRs based on the lower-priced Japanese stocks often combine five or ten shares into each ADR, thus yielding a price high enough to look respectable to a U.S. investor. (At the yen equivalent of $10 per share, Yamaha is reasonably credible. Isuzu, during the same period, was trading at about $4.80, Nippon Steel Corporation at $6.)

Prices on the Frankfurt exchange, by contrast, tend to be much higher than NYSE prices. On Sept. 19, for example, with Henkel trading at 466.50 marks ($249.33) per share, Deutsch Bank stands at 509.50 marks ($272.31), Daimler-Benz at 699.00 marks ($373.60), and Münchener Ruckversicherungs-Gesellschaft (Muench Rueck) at 2,135.00 ($1,140)! These large per-share prices, however, are coupled with smaller trading units—a typical round lot on the Frankfurt exchange is 50 shares.

But Frankfurt prices look quite modest compared to those on the Zurich exchange. Take Ciba, for example. At the previous week's price of 3,230 francs per share and an exchange rate of .6325 U.S. dollars per franc, a share of Ciba costs $2,042.98.

3,230 Sw.francs/sh. × .6325 $US/franc = $2,042.975/sh.

Looking at the previous week's closing price for Ciba provides a lesson in currency exchange. Though the stock was selling for less—3,205 francs—the franc, at .6402 U.S. dollars, was trading higher. When you combine the effects of the lower price and stronger franc, you find the stock was actually worth more in dollars on the previous Friday:

3,205 francs/sh. × .6402 $US/franc = $2,051.84

Ciba's per share price in francs went up during the week, but its dollar-value went down.

You may have noticed in the Ciba example that we reversed our earlier procedure. Instead of dividing by the foreign currency-dollar rate, we multiplied by the U.S. dollar-equivalent rate. Work the conversion either way you like, and you come out with a gargantuan per-share price on the right-hand side of your equation. Who can afford 100 shares of such a stock? Not to worry: the round lot for a Swiss stock trading at a price that high is five shares. (For really expensive Swiss stocks, a round lot is one share.) So our total outlay for one round lot of Ciba is just over $10,000 ($10,214.88). This is actually less money than we would owe for 1,000 shares of Yamaha (1000 × $10.88 = $10,880.00) or 50 shares of Henkel (50 × $249.33 = $12,466.50).

At this point, after a fair amount of calculating, you have nothing more than a sense of your stock's present price. If you're a technician, you can add to this information by consulting *Investor's Daily* charts on the Swiss, Japanese, and German stock-market indexes. The Swiss index, for example, was up 1.5 percent that day but trading toward the bottom of its 52-week range.

But you're still missing a great deal of information that you would expect to find for securities listed on the NYSE. What, for example, is the 52-week trading range of the stocks in question? It isn't given. Do they pay dividends? You can't tell. Are they trading ex-dividend? You don't know. How many shares traded on Sept. 19? All this information is missing from the U.S. press, and pretty tough to come by for individual U.S. investors.

What you need, then, is a set of questions to ask your broker when you call about a foreign stock. Since salespeople who call you often have, if not a script, at least a list of good "probes" and quick answers to common questions, it seems only fair you should have a few guidelines of your own. You'll find those guidelines below.

Everything You Need to Ask about Foreign Stocks When Using a Foreign Broker

- Is the currency convertible?
- Can I pay you with a check in U.S. dollars, or do I need Australian (Japanese, German, etc.) currency?
- When is settlement?
- Are there any problems that may delay settlement? How long will it take?
- Do I pay and then get a certificate? Or do I hold payment until receiving the certificate?
- Who's at risk for any problems that arise before the trade settles—you or me?

Everything You Need to Ask about Foreign Stocks When Using Any Broker, Foreign or Domestic

- Can I get the certificate?
- How long must I wait for the certificate?
- Until I receive the certificate, who gets the dividends?
- When are dividends paid?
- How do I find out about mergers, acquisitions, and other events that might affect my holdings?
- What is the size of a round lot?
- Is the trade executed immediately or after you receive my payment?
- Do you accept only market orders—or will you accept other types, such as limit and stop orders?
- What is the level of insurance protection for my account?
- What must I do when I want to sell?
- Are there any taxes, special or otherwise, on the transaction, on income, or on capital withdrawal?
- What are the commissions? (Remember, they may be higher outside the United States.)

Summary

If you're getting into foreign stocks by way of ADRs or shares of U.S.-based funds invested internationally, you trade just as you always do. A phone call to your broker or to the mutual fund will suffice to get you into the investment, settlement will occur in five business days, and, if you've bought stock, you can leave the shares with your broker for safekeeping or have the certificates shipped to you. Either way, dividends, reports, proxies, and tax information will arrive in your mailbox on time, in English, and (in the case of dividends) denominated in dollars. Further, if your broker should go bankrupt, SIPC insures your assets against losses up to half a million dollars, of which $100,000 can be in cash.

If you invest in foreign shares or funds not traded as ADRs in the U.S. market, you can use a major domestic retail broker, such as Merrill Lynch, Dean Witter, or Shearson; a money-center bank like Citicorp, Manufacturers Hanover, Bankers Trust, Northern Trust, or Security Pacific; or a foreign bank or broker registered on the exchange where your stock trades. If you choose a domestic institution, you will trade and receive dividends in U.S. dollars, settle in five days, and be protected by SIPC. If, however, you use a foreign institution, you will be subject to the laws and customs of the broker's home country. This may involve you in currency-exchange problems, withholding of foreign taxes, longer settlement times, language difficulties, and lack of insurance should your broker defraud you or go bankrupt. (Taking delivery of the certificate yourself removes broker-dealer financial risk from this list.) The first rule of investment after all, is that risk and reward rise and fall together. And there is, as we shall see in later chapters, tremendous reward potential in countries that are just taking off economically.

Now we have a sense of where to look for a broker-dealer equipped to handle foreign trades, and we're armed with a list of questions to ask the representative. In the next chapter, we'll look at potential disasters—the more obvious potholes to steer around on the road to investment success.

CHAPTER 5

How to Avoid
the Pitfalls

In an old German nursery story called "Hans Guck-in-der-Luft," a boy continues, against all adult warnings, to stare dreamily into space as he walks about. In the end he falls into a pond and drowns. Old German nursery stories are like that. They are meant to scare you—for your own good.

So is this chapter. It's mainly about the downside of foreign investment. But it isn't supposed to keep you from buying foreign stocks, any more than the nursery story aims to keep kids from walking. Any more than those bloody films shown in drivers' education classes are meant to keep us from driving. This chapter is intended to keep you out of accidents, not out of the market.

So, what can go wrong with your foreign investment?

Well, everything. Absolutely everything can go wrong. Risk is real—in anyone's stock market. Whether you're buying U.S. or foreign equities, you're taking a chance. If the business you invest in goes broke, you can lose all the money you put up. (If you buy on margin, you can lose the amount of your loan, too.) In fact, by making a list of all the things that can go wrong in the stock market, you could probably convince yourself to sell all your investments and put your cash in a sock. Come to think of it, a good many investors must have done something rather like that after October 19, 1987.

No question about it, things occasionally go awry. Companies go bankrupt. Broker-dealers go bankrupt. Banks go bankrupt. Stock prices drop 20, 30, 50 percent. Companies fail to declare dividends. Hostile takeovers occur, and greenmail, and poison pills. Insiders manipulate markets. All markets. Settlement systems stop settling.

Investing is not for the faint of heart.

But, then, neither is driving. Or thinking.

So if this chapter scares you, remember its purpose in doing so. And it's only one chapter in a book about the adventure of investing wherever you please. Some of the risks you read about are common to all stock markets. Some are unique to foreign markets—as are some of the rewards described in this book. In fact, not to seem unduly gloomy, we will conclude this chapter with a look at what can go right.

A Trio of Terrors

"Everything" is a little broad. We can divide that into three things: You can pick the wrong country, the wrong currency, or the wrong company. The iron law of investing applies abroad as surely as it does at home: risk and potential reward fall and rise together.

At a minimum, you run the same company risks in foreign as in domestic investment. Your company's earnings may go flat because the industry hits the doldrums or the general economy sinks into recession. You can buy in a fast-growing industry only to have your company's products become obsolete as competitors race past it. Management can misjudge customer demand, mandate overproduction or underproduction, hire too optimistically or too sparingly, fail to train and motivate the work force properly, or mismanage in a myriad of other ways. The company might be plagued by strikes or slowdowns. Customer dissatisfaction could erode your company's sales and ruin its reputation. New owners may take the company over and dismantle it immediately for cash or slowly destroy it simply because they don't understand how it became successful in the first place. Whether you invest within your home country or abroad, you are, in other words, subject to all the human errors and eccentricities that bedevil businesses everywhere, no matter how promising they look at the moment you buy into them.

Information Risk

When you buy into a foreign company, you take on what might be called information risk. In the first place, your invested capital is operating at a distance—which is true, too, if you live in Idaho and invest in Houston Industries, Inc. (Houston Industries), or if you live in Tennessee and own Minnesota Mining and Manufacturing (3M). But your foreign holdings are not only distant, they lie across a border or an ocean or both. You might see the company firsthand once every few years, if you're a globetrotting member of the jet set, the multinational corporate community, or the diplomatic service. But that's not very likely. In the meantime, you and the company exist, so to speak, in different information zones.

News

The information that reaches you from foreign countries passes through a series of filters. At each pass, some of the data is left behind. Or all of it is. Most likely, your newspaper, even if it's *The Washington Post* or *The New York*

Times, doesn't consider the crises and triumphs of foreign companies—let alone their ordinary operations—news fit to print. Nor does your local television news department. Anything picked up from foreign sources will probably be reduced in length and depth. What is filtered out may be something of particular importance to shareholders.

Not only do we get less news about foreign companies, we get it late. This means, for example, that you might not find out about a tender offer until it's too late to take advantage of it. News of a management change might not get to you until a subsequent annual report (and that might not get to you at all). A competitive product might be introduced, and you won't find out—and might not be close enough to evaluate the new product even if you do. Your company could be having problems with distribution or service or product failures, but you probably won't hear about these difficulties. Or you will hear about them, but won't be able to assess their magnitude and won't be close enough to see if your company—or a competitor—is doing anything about them.

And the information problems don't stop there. You and the management of your company may speak different languages. If so, and you haven't invested through an ADR or fund, any reports you are fortunate enough to receive will be incomprehensible. Even if you can read your company's literature, however, it may include less information than a domestic company would be required to publish. Or the information may be complete and in a language you can read, and yet be organized in unfamiliar ways or based on economic and accounting assumptions as foreign as the language they're written in.

P/E Ratios

Take, for example, that staple of stock-market analysis, the P/E ratio. If you're reading about a company and assessing the value of its stock, the P/E ratio is one of the first numbers you'll check. As its name implies, the P/E ratio compares the market price of a stock to the company's annual earnings per share of that stock. A relatively high ratio makes investors nervous, since it indicates the stock is expensive in relation to the firm's profits. To get the P/E ratio back in line, either earnings per share must rise or the price of the stock must fall. So far, so good. But what constitutes a high ratio? Unfortunately, the answer to that question varies enormously from country to country—and from time to time. Even the experts don't know quite what to make of the differences.

In Japan, for example, the ratios tend to run much higher than they do in the United States. At this writing, Nippon Telegraph and Telephone Corporation, one of Japan's most powerful companies, sports a P/E ratio higher than 200 to 1. This is by no means the highest P/E ratio on the Tokyo Exchange, though it is above the average, which is in the 50s. The P/E ratio of American Telephone and Telegraph (AT&T), by contrast, is currently 14 to 1, and the regional phone companies are down around 10 or 12 to 1. Historically, these are fairly typical numbers for U.S. companies. The P/E ratio for the Dow 30 stocks, for example, tends toward the low teens, has been below 10 for long periods, and is considered high at 20.

Precisely what the astronomical Japanese P/E ratios mean is open to interpretation. They are at least in part the result of differences in accounting systems. The Japanese, for example, have more rapid depreciation schedules than Americans do, so they deduct a higher percentage of capital costs from earnings each year. The result is a lower earnings figure and a higher ratio of price to earnings. Nevertheless, even calculating a Japanese company's financial statements on American principles doesn't yield a truly comparable set of numbers. P/E ratios are simply one of a set of interacting variables. No matter how you massage the data, in the end you're still comparing apples and oranges. The trick is to learn to analyze Japanese companies in their own context. That's a little like learning to think (or perhaps to dream) in a foreign language, but it's not impossible. Obviously, somebody is making money in the Japanese stock market. Lots of money. So the problems of analysis aren't insuperable. Again, this is just a warning. If you're assessing foreign companies by comparing their numbers to familiar U.S. numbers, you are, like Hans Guck-in-der-Luft, staring in the wrong direction.

Earnings

Another good story about information risk comes from the United Kingdom, where language barriers shouldn't be a problem. Yet a misunderstanding arising from different business attitudes seems to have soured U.K. investors on some smaller U.S. stocks available on the ISE in London. According to an article in *Forbes,* of 17 smaller U.S. companies that began trading in London after 1984, 15 significantly declined in value by mid 1988.[1] The decline of the dollar figured into these losses, of course. But the souring of British attitudes toward these companies had a different source: the American firms didn't know how to think British. Pricing in the United Kingdom, for example, is based on earnings projections, whereas U.S. pricing relies on earnings history. U.S. companies simply don't take their earnings forecasts as seriously as the British, who become most upset with missed forecasts. When the U.S. firms produced lower earnings than predicted, the British began to mistrust them. Even among businesspeople speaking a common language, severe communication problems do arise.

So, in addition to the perils of domestic investment, add to your list of global investment worries another entry—information risk, the problem of finding and interpreting facts and opinions about your foreign investment.

Currency Exchange Risk

We've looked into currency exchange and talked about its potential positive effects. In the mid 1980s, in fact, the story was mostly upbeat for U.S. investors with foreign portfolios. The decline of the dollar combined with growth in other economies to reward Americans in the global market. But this will not be a permanent fixture of international investing. Exchange rates will fluctuate in the future—in both directions. This will mean that sometimes a rise in stock price will be wiped out by an adverse shift in currency values.

Let's look, for example, at what happened to Japanese investors buying shares in U.S. companies during the bull market of the mid 1980s. (From their perspective, U.S. stocks are foreign investments.) These investors might well have seen their stocks double in value as they are measured on Wall Street—in dollars. But those dollars might, in the meantime, have declined 50 percent in value against the yen. A share of McDonald's, for example, selling for about $30 in mid 1985, reached a high of just over $60 before the crash in 1987. Marvelous!

Unfortunately for the Japanese investor who owned McDonald's stock over that period, the dollar declined from an exchange value of about 250 yen in mid 1985 to about 130 yen late in 1987. The stock was worth about twice as much per share after two years, but each dollar was worth about half as much in yen. So the value of the stock as the Japanese investor measures it—in yen—was scarcely higher at $60 per share than it was at $30. Stocks that didn't at least double in dollar value over that period would actually have lost money for the Japanese investor. (We hope our hypothetical investor was not overextended in the U.S. market, and was profiting from the solid performance of stocks in Japan.)

In the worst case, stock values and currency values can

decline together, and the foreign investor suffers a double whammy. Does this situation ever occur? Yes, indeed. That's exactly what happened in the U.S. In late 1987, when the stock market and the dollar went downhill one after the other like Jack and Jill. At that time, our imaginary Japanese investor would have sadly watched his or her U.S. portfolio decline in dollar value even as those dollars declined in yen value. IBM, for example, dropped in value in late 1987 from almost $160 per share (its highest high in October) to just over $100 a share (its lowest low in December). At the same time, the dollar's value slid from 147 yen at its high in October to about 122 yen at its low in December. To have your stock lose about one-third of its value in two months, while the currency it's priced in loses one-sixth of its value, is to have insult added to injury.

All of which brings us to the relationship of share prices and currency values. For learning purposes, it has been worthwhile to separate the two items to make unfamiliar calculations as simple as possible. But in the real world, as you might have suspected, an alteration in exchange rate is going to reverberate throughout the economy.

To illustrate this currency–economy connection, let's look again at the United States. In the past, the strength of the dollar against other currencies has been a problem for U.S. exporters, because it made American goods expensive in foreign markets. The weakening of the dollar during the latter part of the Reagan administration, therefore, was good for such companies: it made their products more competitive in foreign markets. This meant better times for U.S. exporters, and that made for higher stock prices.

A situation that is good for U.S. exporters is, naturally, bad for their competitors. Let's say those exporters were selling casual clothes in Europe in competition with European manufacturers. As the dollar declines in value against European currencies, those U.S. pants and jackets become less expensive relative to the domestic products. And at the lower prices, they begin to look a little more desirable to European consumers. As sales of the U.S. items pick up, the European firms begin to lose market share. And earnings. So their P/E ratios drop, their stock prices follow, and U.S. investors who took positions in those stocks to profit from strengthening European currencies see their investments dropping in price. Are they also dropping in dollar value? That depends, of course, on which happens faster: the rise of the European currency, or the fall of the stock price.

Here's another way in which a weakening dollar can hurt the U.S. investor with an international portfolio. Some foreign businesses depend heavily on exports to the United States. For them, a weak dollar means that their products will cease to be competitive in the American marketplace. In fact, as the dollar declined against the pound and deutsche mark in the mid 1980s, such luxury cars as Porsche and Jaguar lost significant portions of their crucial U.S. market. In such cases, the calculations became rather complex for the U.S. investor.

Let's work it out. The increasing strength of the pound and mark is good, since it means any money made on investment in Porsche AG (Porsche), or Jaguar stock translates into more and more dollars. But it may also be bad, because it means that Porsches and Jaguars will become so costly in dollars that they may be priced out of the crucial U.S. market. Moreover, any dollars that the car manufacturers make in the U.S. will be worth less when translated into pounds and marks at home. The woes of the company will be reflected in falling stock prices. And then the investor's success or failure depends on which moves faster — the rising value of the dollar, or the falling value of the stock.

So you can invest in a country whose currency is appreciating and still get burned, depending on the company you select. When you're considering foreign investment, then, ask yourself about the potential effect of currency changes on the economy in general and your industry and company in particular. Look carefully at the condition of a country's currency, at the currency's prospects for strengthening or weakening against your own money, and at the impact of changing currency values on the profits of the companies that interest you.

Along with the exchange rate, you also need to consider the extent to which a currency is convertible and exportable. Not all countries allow their currency to flow freely into other currencies and other countries. This situation in any given country is subject to change, and so is anything written here. At the moment, Thailand, Jamaica, and Italy place restrictions on the flow of their currencies.

Let's consider what such restrictions on the Italian lira might mean for an investor interested in Italian stocks. As Italy and other European countries move, step by step, toward the full integration of the Common Market in 1992, the lira will become fully interchangeable with other currencies. A potential investor in Italy will want to ask how this might affect the Italian economy in general and what impact it will have on particular industries and businesses. Will lira flow suddenly out of the country—into Swiss banks just across the border, for example, Or will other currencies flow into Italy? What will either situation mean for Italy's banks? For banks in nearby cities and countries? This leads us to consider the overall prospects for Italy as a potential source of risk for our investment.

Country Risk—a.k.a. Sovereign Risk

As the Common Market countries dismantle all obstacles to trade, including customs and tariffs as well as currency

restrictions, will Italian businesses tend to thrive or dis-
integrate? At the moment, predictions point both ways.
Some economists contend that Italy, with a reputation for
stock-exchange corruption and widespread black-market
activity, will fare poorly in the new, open Europe. Others
believe that Italy is alive with creativity and enterprise,
not to mention the attractions of its coasts and climate,
and that businesses will take advantage of the opportunity
to migrate southward—as U.S. corporations migrated toward the southern states in the 1970s. One thing is certain:
change is coming to Italy and to the rest of Europe—change
that makes everything else uncertain. The situation is filled
with peril and potential for investors.

Imagine a corporation that you would be especially
eager to invest in: solid management, huge marketshare,
a product you understand and trust. Now try to picture
that corporation operating in different countries. Think of
the ways that your ideal company's business might be
damaged if you place it inside the wrong borders—where
the work force is untrained or unmotivated; where raw
materials are unavailable; where taxes are onerous, trans-
portation is poorly developed, the climate is hostile, or the
political situation uncertain.

Let's look first at potential political problems—the misfortunes that might befall your ideal company because of
governmental decisions. Changing tariffs and customs,
mentioned in regard to Italy, present one example of political actions that can harm the value of your investments.
And what we said of Italy, with appropriate modifications,
applies throughout the Common Market. In their movement
toward true market unification in 1992, these countries will
institute changes that may have profound effects on themselves and on their present trading partners. What if you
invest in a company that has benefited from the barriers?
Perhaps its products sell locally, in a market previously

protected from foreign competition. Will it survive when the barriers fall?

Or perhaps you invest in a company in another part of the world—a New Zealand wool exporter, for instance—that relies on having buyers in Europe. What will happen when European nations begin to rely on one another for markets? Perhaps Scottish wool will become an unbeatable competitor in such an atmosphere. Of course, it could work the other way instead. Perhaps a more open and integrated Europe will become a larger marketplace for the world's goods. Either way, change means risk—as well as opportunity. And the Common Market countries are undergoing long-term, profound political change—sometimes in ways that aren't obvious.

Temporal Risk

Consider, for example, time—an unexpected barrier to the economic integration of Europe. Though the continent spans only two time zones, the way different countries organize their workdays may create substantial problems for transnational business. While the British get off to a slow start in the mornings, Scandinavians are up and working early. The Swiss and French are, in some cases, meeting for business breakfasts—with croissants, of course. In southern Europe, schedules are generally looser, sometimes including an afternoon siesta. And people can be most resistant to changes in their scheduling.

The Greek socialist government of Andreas Papandreou tried banning the traditional three-hour afternoon siesta—with plenty of logical justification. They argued, for example, that closing business from 2 to 5 P.M. creates two extra rush hours—with attendant increases in pollution. It also cuts into the tourist trade by closing stores during prime shopping hours. After months of grumbling, Greek citizens succeeded in restoring the siesta. The politics of the afternoon break will no doubt effect the ability of Greece to thrive in a more unified Europe. When Greeks pause for lunch may, along with weightier items in world news, affect your portfolio. And so many other deep-rooted traditions.

Fear of Foreigners

Business may be rational. Politicians may respond to the expressed needs of business leaders and investors. But logic—which suggests seeking the best markets for one's goods and services and investing where the returns are highest and safest—is not all that nations live by. Americans, too, are possessed by fears and affinities that run deeper than economic rationality. Presidential candidates play on our distrust of foreigners when they decry the Japanese and European ownership of U.S. real estate, corporations, and government debt. If such ethnic hostility is politically potent in a large, wealthy nation peopled by immigrants from around the world, imagine the fear of foreign investment experienced by smaller nations without ethnically diverse cultures.

Take South Korea, for instance. Fear of U.S. influence runs so high there that demonstrators harass patrons and owners of theaters where U.S. movies are showing. To disrupt the movie *Fatal Attraction*, saboteurs released snakes (harmless ones) in the theater restrooms.

From the Greek's rather endearing devotion to the siesta, through the downright frightening antipathy of some Koreans to U.S. movies, nontariff trade barriers will bedevil global investors in the future. Simply put, an investor's money is not always welcome abroad, even where it may be needed.

Market Manipulation

Along with afternoon naps and snakes, market manipulation can be a problem for investors—domestic or foreign. Though all markets are manipulated, some are more manipulated than others. One country's manipulation is another's fair practice. Insider trading is strictly forbidden and strongly sanctioned in the United States. That does not mean it doesn't happen here. The market danced to the tune called by Ivan Boesky and his cohorts for years before they were caught and stopped. Nor is this by any means the only instance of U.S. insiders' using privileged information to increase their own wealth at public expense. Imagine, then, what manipulations occur in other countries —virtually all other countries—where insider trading is unsanctioned.

Market manipulation is a variety of information risk. A foreign investor is twice an outsider in markets that take insider trading for granted. Insiders have the best information. Domestic investors have the next best. Foreign investors are more or less in the dark—at least in regard to fast-breaking news. This lack of timely information makes it very risky to invest for short-term gains in markets outside your own country (where short-term risk is scarcely inconsequential).

Government and Politics

In the case of insider trading, legislators and regulators have a potentially positive role to play in improving your luck at international investing. But legislators are not always the good guys—from the investor's point of view. In the creation of havoc, politicians can be endlessly inventive. The pressures brought to bear on them, of course, are intense, conflicting, and not all designed to enhance the wealth of overseas investors. An apparently friendly political environment can turn troublesome quite unexpectedly.

As this is being written, for example, the government of Taiwan is struggling with the investment community about the capital gains tax. For over a decade, capital gains were not taxed—a most favorable circumstance in a rampant bull market. By late October of 1988, the stock market had climbed 276 percent since the beginning of the year, and, without warning, the government reimposed the capital gains tax at rates up to 50 percent on assets held less than one year. Unfortunately for investors who wanted to get out of the market in a hurry, regulations allow a stock's price to vary no more than 3 percent per day. As a *Barron's* article put it, "When everyone rushes for the exit at once, few escape."[2] In response to investors' outrage (and the stock market debacle) the government raised the amount of gain exempt from taxation. As investors are at risk from the machinations of governments, so governments are reciprocally vulnerable to the acts and outcries of investors.

The changing of governments, or a change of plans by a stable government, can mean disaster for investors. Or it can bring a bonanza. In the United States, the accession of the Kennedy administration in 1960 heralded an economic boom, as did the inauguration of a very different style of administration in 1980. After a dramatically unpleasant start, the Thatcher government in England pulled off what now looks like an economic miracle to some—or, from the back-bencher's vantage point, like an economic shell game.

Anticipating the effect a new government may have on the economy is something less than scientific. Politics is based upon disagreement: as in the Thatcher example, the governing party sees an obvious miracle where the opposition sees fiscal sleight-of-hand. Indeed, sometimes governments that appear to be the surest allies of investors

Figure 5-1. Economic Growth Rates

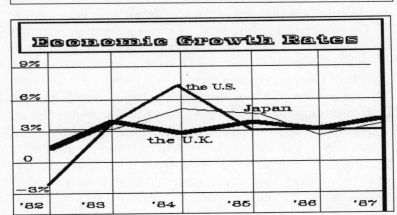

Courtesy of *Fortune* Magazine.

suddenly move in ways that seem mysterious even—or especially—to their free-enterprise fans. "The government's whole free-market policy is showing itself to be either confused or shallow,"[3] complained one investment firm's energy-research director when Prime Minister Thatcher demanded cutbacks in Kuwait's share of British Petroleum. The government, of course, maintained that the shift in policy on foreign investment actually affirmed free-market principles by reducing British involvement in the Organization of Petroleum Exporting Countries (OPEC) cartel.

Whether an investor can successfully negotiate political risk in a foreign country is a matter of conjecture. On the one hand, distance decreases one's access to pertinent information. On the other hand, it may provide a more objective perspective than the insider has. The fact remains that government actions sometimes have immediate and highly detrimental consequences for one's portfolio.

During the late 1960s, the Indonesian government delighted industry and investors by laying plans to develop the tiny island of Batam, which lies southeast of the city-state of Singapore, just over a half-hour's trip away by ferry. About two-thirds the size of Singapore, Batam lies close to strategic shipping lanes. Unlike Singapore, it is virtually undeveloped. To rectify that situation, the Indonesian government signed contracts with Pertamina, the national oil company, and with several of the company's foreign partners.

In apparent support of its grand intentions for Batam, the government, in the early 1970s, declared the island an industrial zone, and Pertamina adopted a plan to develop the facilities and infrastructure necessary to make Batam a hub of international economic activity. Roads were built, telecommunications established, an airport constructed, and ambitious plans outlined for refineries, warehouses, manufacturing, tourism, and other enterprises.

Unfortunately, Batam remains something less than a second Singapore in the late 1980s, having experienced several of the difficulties that plague developing economies. Rising oil prices and the decline of the U.S. dollar brought recession. A scandal led to the ouster of Pertamina's president. Officials became concerned that foreign investment in Batam, especially from Singapore, would lead to foreign domination of the island. And time was lost in developing a new plan after the Pertamina scandal derailed the first one.[4]

Are there other country risks? Indeed. Look out for apparent prosperity based on success in a limited number of industries. As an undiversified portfolio puts an investor at the mercy of each stock, an undiversified economy makes a country especially vulnerable to low points in the business cycle. Jamaica, for example, was relatively prosperous in recent years until its tourist trade collapsed. The government took steps to revive tourism, but then disaster hit Jamaican mining and kept the economy on the ropes. Even the weather has contributed to Jamaican problems with a devastating hurricane season in 1988.

Economies that rely on petroleum, for another example, have ridden a dizzying roller coaster during the last two decades. When oil prices soared in the 1970s, Saudi Arabia, Kuwait, Mexico, Brazil, and Venezuela all found themselves instantly wealthy—relative to their own past conditions. But an economy that lives by the price of oil may also die by the price of oil. And so it happened to oil-rich Mexico and Brazil in the 1980s.

Both nations leveraged their petroleum-based fortunes by borrowing against future revenues, on the assumption that oil prices would continue to skyrocket. They didn't. Instead, OPEC nations couldn't set production limits, a glut developed, the price of oil dropped precipitously, and the inflowing stream of currency dried up. Those who borrowed against the promise of ever-increasing crude oil prices could no longer pay the interest on their loans, let alone the principal. This has created continuing crisis in credit markets as banks and governments pile shaky loan on top of shaky loan to keep such countries as Mexico and Brazil afloat— or drowning in debt, depending on your point of view.

The fate of Panama is another warning sign for international investors. Beware of countries that may run afoul of the U.S. government—or any other major trading partner. Sanctions and trade embargoes can, in some cases, be devastating to a smaller country's economy.

Nationalization

The biggest country risk of all, the bane of the foreign investor (or the domestic investor, for that matter), is nationalization. It happened to the plantations of the United Fruit and Produce Company (United Fruit), the railroads and banks of England, foreign oil leases in Arab countries, and, more recently, to the banks in France. In the developed countries and the emerging nations, in Europe, South America, and the Middle East, we have seen governments expropriate land, equipment, and buildings from the investors whose capital financed their purchase and use. Now, as private investors are regaining ownership of enterprises such as railroads and phone companies, we might want to remember that the pendulum can always swing back during the next political regime.

At the very least, nationalization means a dramatic change in the terms of your investment. The expropriating government may compensate you for your losses, or it may not. If there is compensation, it may be very low. Or it may take the form of bonds with highly discounted value and low coupon rates — something less than a scrupulously fair deal.

And there you have the worst of it — the things that can go wrong — from hurricanes to nationalization. Some of these misfortunes are shared by domestic and foreign investors — weather is weather, wherever you invest. Some, such as information risk and nationalization, seem unique to foreign markets. There is no way to protect yourself from all risk. But there certainly are ways to minimize your dangers. Chapters 6, 7, and 8 focus on strategies to help you choose wisely. Now, however, it's time to move on to happier possibilities — to the reasons that drew you to the subject of foreign investment in the first place.

Rewards

What can go right? Everything. An investment success story is just the mirror image of a disaster: you can select a successful company in a rapidly growing and politically stable country with a strengthening currency.

Picking a country may not be your first consideration in the investment process, but that decision can be crucial to your success. In the past, you probably haven't consciously considered country selection as a part of investing. But you've been selecting a country right along—your own. Now that we're all becoming increasingly aware of foreign investment possibilities, and of the global dimensions of so many blue chip companies, it's harder to ignore the international alternatives. You may still decide—for economic or moral reasons—that your home country is the best place to invest. But that should now be a conscious decision—a choice, not an imperative

The Right Government

For the moment, imagine you have invested your money in a foreign stock. What must happen for you to feel you've done the right thing? Certainly you want the government to pursue policies favorable to the economy in general—and to your company and industry in particular. You hope, of course, for a stable government. No doubt you would find a succession of military coups most unsettling. Most of us, for ethical as well as financial reasons, want our money to be invested in a well-run, stable, reasonably free country where the leaders live in harmony with the citizens.

While reasonable investors might disagree about the details of a sound economic policy, all would concur that the country they invest in should look favorably upon business, should promote fair investment practices, and should not exclude or inhibit foreign investment by discriminatory regulations and taxes. Things have gone right for you as a foreign investor, then, if you've selected a country that is eager to see your money put to work in its economy; has a fair, efficient, predictable investment market; and is governed in the best interests of all its citizens. And you want your money in a country at peace with its neighbors.

118

The Right Economy

Beyond politics, there is the state of the economy. As there are growth companies, so, too, are there growth countries —nations in which your invested capital can multiply rapidly. The economy of an emerging nation can sustain more rapid expansion than is possible for the economy of a highly developed nation. They are racing to catch up. Naturally this rapid growth potential is linked to greater risk.

The rapid reconstruction of Japan is one of the better-known wonders of the modern world. Perhaps less well known has been the growth of the other East Asian nations, including Singapore, Hong Kong, Taiwan, and Korea. On the average, those four economies experienced 10 percent annual growth between 1965 and 1973, and, from 1973 to 1987, 7.7 percent yearly growth—double Japan's, triple that of the countries of the Organization for Economic Cooperation and Development (OECD). Extrapolating from recent rates of growth, economists predict that East Asia may by the end of the century have a combined gross national product greater than Europe's and equal to North America's.[5] Other, longer-term estimates postulate a growth of 3 percent in the U.S. economy, 7 percent in China and India, 5 percent in East Asia and Latin America. In 25 years, this would reduce the U.S. share of world GNP from one-fourth to one-sixth.[6]

Of course, events have a way of making fools of forecasters, and the world in 10 or 25 years may bear little resemblance to what we now foresee. No doubt you will consider yourself to have picked wisely if you invest in a country that constantly increases its share of global wealth.

If 5 to 7 percent stable annual growth doesn't excite you, imagine the effect this can have on a country's stock market and on its infant industries. The long bull market of the 1980s had impressive consequences around the world. But markets rose at substantially different rates.

During 1986, for instance, while the U.S. market rose 18.6 percent, Australian and Japanese stocks shot up by 47.6 percent and 49.7 precent respectively. From early 1986 to the peak in 1987, the Singapore stock market nearly tripled in value. During the bull market of 1982 to 1987, the Hong Kong market, as measured by the Hang Seng Index, charged upward from a low of under 700 to a high around 4,000—very nearly a 500 percent increase. And that was on top of an increase of about 700 percent in the years since the nadir in 1974.

Clearly, we're looking at best cases here, and the statistics could be used to tell other, less inspiring stories. But we've already covered the worst cases. The point is: these numbers may be fantastic, but they are not fantasies. The greatest possibility of rapid growth exists when a country has the most room to grow. At takeoff, an economy can pick up speed like a rocket. At higher altitudes, it's more likely to reach cruising speed and level off.

The Right Currency

Amid all this political and economic happiness, as you know from chapter 3, you have to keep watch on the currency exchange rates. In the best of all possible investment worlds, political stability, leapfrogging GNP gains, and a buoyant stock market will be augmented by strengthening of the currency. We already know that the value of the U.S. dollar tended downward against many other currencies in the middle of the 1980s. Foreign investors saw any gains in stock price magnified by the favorable exchange rate. While the Nikkei Index was soaring so majestically in 1986 and 1987, the yen was doubling in value against the dollar—and thereby doubling any gains the U.S. investor made in Japanese stocks. Figures 5-2 and 5-3 show the rising value of the yen in 1986 and 1987, and the soaring performance of the Tokyo Exchange.

Figure 5–2. Yen/dollar exchange rate, 1986–88

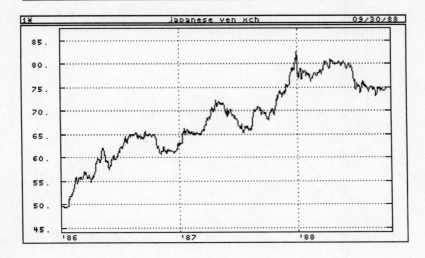

Figure 5–3. The Nikkei Index, 1986–88

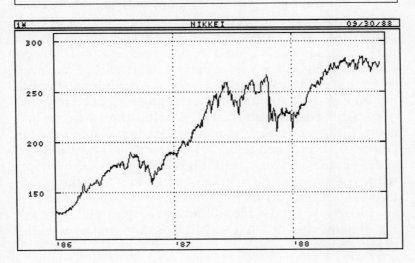

Figure 5–4. The Nikkei Index in U.S. dollars, 1985–88

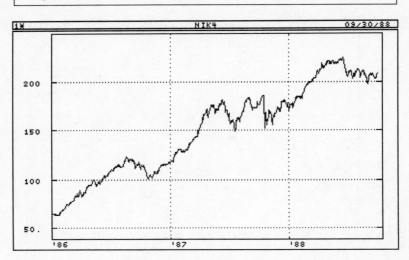

Of course, your happiness as an investor rests finally on successful stock selection. While a rising economic tide may tend to lift all companies, some will float higher than others. If things go right, your money will be in those companies that outperform the general market, growth companies in a growth country. Your investment in Honda ADRs, for instance, would have appreciated about 700 percent in the eight years from early 1980 to early 1988 (even including the October 1987 crash!)—a combined effect of favorable politics, rising GNP, strengthening currency, and successful corporate strategy. During the same period, every 1,000 yen you invested in Matsushita would have become 6,000 yen—and that 500 percent gain is not adjusted to reflect the exchange rate! Figure 5–4 shows the performance of Japanese stock prices quoted in U.S. dollars from late 1985 through 1988.

Clearly, it is possible that everything can go right for the global investor. Just as it is possible that everything can go wrong.

Summary

Investing in another country is a bit like moving there. For better or worse, your finances become involved in the fate of the nation—subject to fluctuations in the currency, elections, coups, and revolutions, taxation, invasions from across the border, the agonies of cultural change, the vicissitudes of weather, and the cycles of the economy. You aren't just a tourist any longer when you assume ownership in another country's economy. This is both exciting and a little scary. Choose your new country carefully— and with high hopes.

Endnotes

1. "Small Isn't Necessarily Beautiful," Richard C. Morais, *Forbes*, May 30, 1988, p. 270.

2. "Ooh-la-la, Sassoon . . . Taiwan Tumbles," Peter C. DuBois, *Barron's*, October 3, 1988, p. 65.

3. "Heat is on Britain after demand for Kuwait divestiture," Cotten Timberlake, *Minneapolis Star Tribune*, October 7, 1988, p. 3D.

4. If the story intrigues you, see "Batam Aspires to Become a Mini-Singapore," Dr. Philippe T. Regnier, *Asian Finance*, June 15, 1988, pp. 74–75.

5. See, for example, "Asia's Pacific Rim," David Housego, *The Financial Times*, June 30, 1988.

6. "The Rising Stars," Swan Lee and Tatiana Purschine, *Forbes*, May 5, 1986, p. 109.

CHAPTER 6

Choosing a Country: The Fundamentals

Wilderness campers have compasses and watertight sleeping bags. Astronauts have space suits and a direct line to mission control. High-wire walkers have a flexible pole, an exquisite sense of balance—and, perhaps, a net. Investors have analysis.

Investment analysis is of two sorts, fundamental and technical. Fundamental analysis concentrates on digging up and assaying the relevant facts. The fundamental analyst wants to see a company's balance sheet and income statement, to compare indebtedness to assets, discover how much they earn in relation to the price of their stock, and other quantified measures of their likelihood of success. Technical analysts study stock charts hoping to find, in the upward and downward curves, patterns that might extend at least into the near future and thus predict the next price movement. We will look at the uses to which global investors can put each type of analysis: the fundamentalist approach in this chapter, the technical approach in chapter 7.

Five Rules for Global Investors

Picking stocks is an adventure. Like all adventures, it can be undertaken with varying degrees of prudence. The more you learn from studying fundamental or technical data, the more confident you feel about your selections. But in the end it all comes down to making a choice and stepping off into the uncharted future.

One can, in fact, make a completely unreasonable choice and strike it rich. One can also make a perfectly reasonable choice and lose money. You've probably heard about the amateur investment club that decided to invest alphabetically for their stock, beginning with X. They bought Xerox Corporation (Xerox) when it was new on the market. They all became wealthy. That's rather like choosing a country by spinning the globe, stopping it with your finger, and investing in the place you're pointing to. It might work. It would be fun. And you'd learn a lot. Putting your money into a country tends to focus your attention on events there. But to reduce the risk a little, we're suggesting five rules.

Since you're an experienced investor, you've evolved a system of company selection that suits your personality and your means. Those new factors puzzle you, though — foreign currencies and politics and languages and customs. Different settlement procedures. Unfamiliar accounting conventions. You know that the entire market is important, not just the particular company. You want to pick a company in a prosperous country, because you've seen the tendency of a bull market in the United States to take your stocks up, and you've seen your investments dragged down by the weight of a bear market. You simply need to adapt your system of selecting domestic stocks to meet the new challenges of selecting foreign companies. And that's where the five rules come in. Now we'll look at each of the rules in turn.

Table 6-1. Rules of the Game

Rule 1:	Establish a 10 percent minimum
Rule 2:	Invest long term
Rule 3:	Know the company
Rule 4:	Know the country
Rule 5:	Know yourself

Rule 1: Establish a 10 Percent Minimum

Comfort varies from investor to investor, and from time to time, but as a general rule, we think you should have at least 10 percent of your money in foreign markets. At first, that minimum should probably be your maximum as well. As you grow more familiar with overseas markets, your comfort level may rise. Some advisors suggest, in fact, that proper diversification requires all of us to keep 15 percent of our money outside domestic markets. The type of investment may also influence your decision: putting 15 percent of your capital into global or international funds may not disturb your sleep as much as sinking 10 percent into one or two foreign companies. So here is a corollary to the first rule: diversify your international investments — as you do your domestic portfolio. Investment-company shares can help you do this. But if you have sufficient capital, you can be your own global fund, selecting stocks from several different countries.

Rule 2: Invest Long Term

Get in for years, not for weeks or even months. You may be tempted to go for short-term gains. Foreign markets, with their sometimes startling volatility, certainly offer the potential for overnight appreciation. But you're not very likely to be able to take advantage of that volatility. Why?

Communications problems, for one thing. You may have a broker in New Zealand, for example, who speaks your language and forwards your annual reports in English. But in New Zealand, nestled up against the international dateline, it's already tomorrow.

When it's two o'clock in the afternoon for your New Zealand broker, you're watching the prime time TV programs of the night before. Or you're bowling, or reading *War and Peace,* or whatever you do in the evening. So your broker may not feel like ringing you up with the latest takeover news—if you're speculating for short-term gains on a possible buyout. If she doesn't get around to calling you until noon the next day, you're on the subway looking for the exit that leads to your favorite martini. And you're a long way off, and your broker is busy prospecting, and your New Zealand holdings aren't a major part of her business anyway, and so on. You've played telephone tag with someone across town. Factor in 17 time zones and you get the idea about overseas communications. And if you don't have a foreign broker or other informant to call you with instant updates, you're at the mercy of the media. When is the last time your newspaper or television network brought you fast-breaking news of events in Wellington, New Zealand? So don't play a long-distance corporate takeover game. By the time you hear the news in this country, the negotiations may be complete—or they may have fallen through.

You need patience in the international marketplace. Patience to learn the rules of the game as it is played in other markets. Patience to gather the information you need to assure yourself that a particular company and country are worth your investment dollars. Patience to wait for the appropriate time to buy the stocks you like. Patience to ride out the inevitable downturns in the market and the economy.

The long-range tendency of stock markets is upward: that's a major attraction of equity investing. But the generally uphill ride does not run smoothly and steadily in one direction—as if you were climbing the unvarying slope of a mountain. It leads, instead, through a series of foothills. You go up awhile, then you maintain your position. Then you go downhill. Then you move along the floor of the valley for a time. Then you move uphill again. On the average, you're gaining altitude; but you aren't always higher than where you were last week, last month, or even last year. Figures 6–1 through 6–3 show long-term stock-market trends in Canada, Japan, and the United Kingdom.

It's that average gain that you try to capture in your international investments—not the briefer, more explosive gains that are interspersed with shorter declines along the way. You need patience not to sell every time the stock price—or the value of the currency—levels off or drops.

Rule 3: Know the Company

This rule, appropriately, has three corollaries:

> All recommendations are questionable.
> All markets are manipulated.
> All numbers are manipulated.

You saw "all markets are manipulated" in chapter 5. It's worth repeating. Notice again the fact that this corollary, like the other two, begins with *All*. Rule 3 applies in the United States as well as the rest of the world.

The Company

In essence, Rule 3 advises you not to turn your decisions over to someone else—someone with a hot tip, for example, or all the investors running up a stock's price, or the analysts and accountants who massage the numbers on

Figure 6–1.   Canada, 1945–88: U.S. Commerce Department data

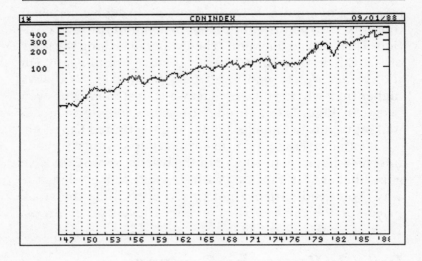

Figure 6–2.   Japan, 1947–88: U.S. Commerce Department data

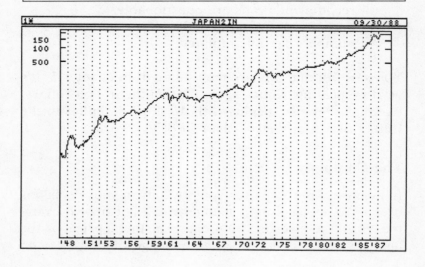

Figure 6–3. U.K., 1944–88: U.S. Commerce Department data

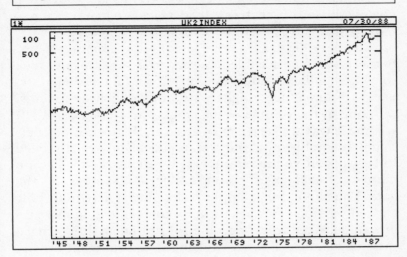

financial statements. Do a little checking on your own and exercise some caution. You want a company that suits your goals, not someone else's. This may mean selecting a company because it's in a business you understand, because it has the proper size and diversification, because its growth patterns correspond to your financial goals and risk tolerance, because you trust its management philosophy, or because it meets other criteria you ordinarily apply.

Even if you like the company generally, check to see how its growth patterns may be affected by its market. This is especially important when the stock looks too good to be true. Start by putting the market's present performance into historical perspective. If prices have gone up 800 percent in the last three years, perhaps the market is due to turn around soon. Unfortunately, it is easy to nod sagely and say that what goes up must come down. Predicting how far up it will go, when it will stop, and how far it will fall

131

is much harder. (One could say that, like all crystal-ball gazing, it's impossible.) But you certainly do yourself a favor if you look for extreme tendencies in a market's direction before you get on board.

Compare the stock's price history to the market index. Is there some noticeable discrepancy? Is your hot stock soaring in a flat or down market? If so, find out what unusual circumstances might justify the bullish sentiments.

Look at the volume of the stock you're considering. If volume is way up, be wary. In general, there's nothing particularly intelligent about a stampede. But you also need to be wary of volume numbers. When stocks trade on a number of exchanges, no one collects and integrates the data. You might, for example, be looking at data that show a rapidly rising stock price but no corresponding increase in volume. What would account for this anomaly? Perhaps the stock trades on other exchanges and rampant buying in other countries is running up the price. And you don't know what is prompting that surge of interest.

The Marketplace

Each marketplace has its own peculiar set of customs. Consider these customs when you evaluate foreign stocks.

In some markets, broker-dealers pursue a stock-of-the-week approach — which leads to the sudden increase in volume we just warned you about. You probably aren't interested in buying a stock whose popularity is bound to peak before next Monday.

Does this sound like blatant manipulation? It is. Be realistic about markets: manipulation is always possible. One experienced manager of international accounts, who is even more successful than he is cynical, follows stocks in several countries with frankly manipulated markets. He buys when the market is quiet, waits for the manipulators to move in, and sells when the stock is touted to him.

Success for him is based on guessing where manipulation is most likely to strike next.

As an international investor, you might find some comfort in the idea that manipulation occurs in all markets, not just the smaller or newer ones. From this perspective, investing in foreign stocks doesn't suddenly open you up to a risk you didn't run before. Nor does investing only in the United States guarantee that you'll never be blindsided by, say, insider trading. It's a matter of degree.

The fact is, though, you probably are less likely to be the victim of manipulation in the U.S. stock market, where you are protected by Treasury Department watchdogs; by the congressionally mandated SEC; by the exchanges, which police member firms; by the NASD, which casts a baleful eye on the practices of OTC firms; and by compliance departments within broker-dealers. Not to mention Ralph Nader and the journalists on "60 Minutes." But larceny springs eternal, and is sometimes perpetrated with great cunning—right under the noses of regulators.

The infamous Ivan Boesky, for example, built a network of insider connections that allowed him to invest in firms about to be involved in acquisitions. Those on the other side of Boesky's trades were taken for a ride. Clearly, it is possible to garner and profit from inside information even in the United States—at least for a time. Though the capture and punishment of those involved may buttress one's faith in the system, it also warns us that the system is vulnerable. If one Boesky is possible, are there others who have not been caught?

And if a Boesky can prosper amid all the computer trails, regulations, and sanctions in the United States, imagine how much greater is the likelihood that Boeskys are thriving where there are no watchdogs. And if you feel some anger at being had in the United States, where the law is on your side, imagine how you might feel about discovering you've been duped in a market that takes that sort of thing for granted—Taiwan, for example. Or Italy. Or even Japan. You might feel you'd been had by the entire country, not just by a few unscrupulous traders.

Throughout 1988 and into 1989, the Japanese have been wrestling with a stock-market scandal that has forced the resignation of a number of eminent politicians, including the prime minister. With the assistance of insiders, political aides were able to purchase stock in Recruit Cosmos Co. (Recruit), before the public and below the offering price. It was a method of fund raising. Those involved have suffered from tarnished reputations and lost jobs. But they have not been taken to court, because they broke no securities laws. If they received their cheap shares in return for favors, they are guilty of taking bribes. But receiving the stock ahead of the public is not illegal. Perhaps legislation is forthcoming, since the revelation of the practice has precipitated a scandal. But will laws be the end of insider trading? U.S. history suggests otherwise. To keep up with the creativity of the devious, U.S. regulators have continuously been forced to expand the definition of unfair manipulation.

Classic manipulation of the market is clearly selfish, intended to drive prices up or down so the perpetrator benefits at the expense of others. Not all manipulation is so obviously ill-intended. Indeed, markets these days are routinely manipulated in the name of the general welfare—at least, for the general welfare of one nation or another. Whether any particular investor thinks such tampering is fair and beneficial is perhaps another matter. Black Monday, for example, almost certainly happened in part because of efforts to control the relative values of currencies—especially the dollar, which since 1985 had been declining in value against other major currencies. That decline itself was a product of an explicit policy (manipulation, in other words) agreed upon by the so-called Group of Seven, a council of leading Western industrial nations.

What was the point of this policy? Letting the dollar drop in value was one way of attacking the U.S. balance-of-payments problem. The less the dollar is worth, the cheaper U.S. products are in other countries — and the more competitive. By the same token, a weakening of the dollar raises the price to Americans of goods imported into the United States, and therefore makes them less competitive. The combination of more competitively priced U.S. exports and less competitive imports should lead to improvement in the U.S. balance of payments: less money going out of the country to pay for imports, more money coming into the country to pay for exports.

In early 1987, the Group of Seven decided that the dollar had dropped far enough and the payment problem was turning around. The nations then began cooperating to raise the dollar's value. Unfortunately, the balance-of-payments problem stubbornly refused to go away, and the consensus among the seven manipulators broke down. In October, Germany announced that it would no longer cooperate in propping up the dollar at the expense of its own currency and economy. The Germans were worried about inflation, as were other Group of Seven countries. In anger, U.S. Treasury Secretary James Baker declared that we would not bear the burden of propping up the dollar alone — the Treasury had been raising U.S. interest rates to make dollar-denominated bonds more attractive.

Paradoxically, perhaps, Baker's remarks were construed as harbingers of inflation. The news that the dollar's value was likely to keep falling led investors around the world to believe that U.S. interest rates would rise (to counteract the dollar's weakness) and inflation overtake the U.S. economy, with consequent weakening of corporate earnings. Lower corporate earnings would depress the value of corporate stock. These bearish sentiments contributed to worldwide selling of U.S. stocks, culminating in the wholesale slaughter on October 19.[1]

135

The moral of our complicated tale is relatively simple: all markets are manipulated by governments and their central banks—sometimes for the good of all nations, sometimes only for the (perceived) good of one nation. It's not just insiders in Taipei or Tokyo or Milan who bear watching when you're risking your capital in the equity markets. No doubt the U.S. decision to let the dollar continue sinking was perceived to be in the public interest, but try selling that idea to someone who stayed in the market through the meltdown!

There may be an ironic sequel to this story. In his book *Black Monday, Wall Street Journal* writer Tim Metz asserts that stock-market officials and the U.S. government may have intervened on Tuesday to stop the market before it collapsed. Using as evidence a minute-by-minute record of Tuesday's events, Metz proves to his own satisfaction (if circumstantially) that stock-exchange president John Phelan, with the cooperation of NYSE specialists and the Chicago Board of Trade (CBT), resuscitated the collapsing DJIA by running up the price of the CBT's Major Market Index, and then, for apparent confirmation of an uptrend, by buying enough of the thirty industrial stocks to lift the DJIA as well. Metz further concludes that the market conspirators were supported in their benign manipulations by the White House, the FRB, and the SEC.

Inquiries into the events surrounding Black Monday have politely overlooked the possibility of such official manipulation: "You don't want to put people in jail for saving the market," as a member of the Senate Banking Committee said.[2] One could argue, on the other hand, that the market if left alone might have "saved" itself. Or one could say, with consistent free-market logic, that markets do not benefit in the long run from near-term fixes. Those who had taken short positions in expectation of continued declines might legitimately ask who was saved from what. In any case, manipulators may have the best intentions and no desire for personal profit. But from good intentions or bad, all markets, as we said, are manipulated.

The Numbers

All numbers are manipulated, too. Balance sheets, income statements, and the ratios based on them—the staples of fundamental analysis—are all subject to manipulation. In the United States, corporations distribute two separate reports. One informs shareholders of the level of annual earnings; the other goes to the IRS to establish tax liability. In Japan and many other countries, corporations distribute only one report on taxes and earnings. Recognizing that corporations calculate their earnings in different ways (and for different audiences) is not to argue that fundamental analysis is a waste of time when studying a foreign firm. By all means, look at the P/E ratio, the dividend yield, the company's indebtedness, cash flow, the value of its assets, and its projected profits. Study all available information. The trick is to avoid comparing an orange to an apple and conclude that it's a lemon. As we said earlier, a P/E ratio in Japan simply does not have the same meaning as a P/E ratio in the United States—or in any other country.

When you're interpreting a number, you need to find the proper context. If, for example, you're looking at an Italian automobile manufacturer, don't compare its numbers to the general marketplace in the United States, or even to U.S. automakers. First, make historical comparisons: how does the P/E ratio (or debt ratio or whatever) look in comparison to historic highs and lows for that company? If it's very high, take that as a warning sign. Then try a comparison with other Italian companies—especially those in similar situations. Get as close as you can to comparing oranges with oranges, apples with apples.

And bear in mind that fundamental analysis is tricky enough even when you stay within one system and have a good grasp of that system's rules. We place great faith in numbers; they seem clear and indisputable. Words we find less reassuring, more subject to error and falsification. But numbers, too, are tokens in games played for profit. In the United States, for example, companies may deduct their research and development expenses in the current year, or they may spread the deductions over several years. One dollar amount of expenses, therefore, can translate into different yearly deductible amounts. The less deducted for expenses, the higher the annual earnings figure. And a higher earnings figure means a lower P/E ratio. There is no lying here, but there is manipulation.

Despite their apparent precision, numbers are often mere estimates. Banks are required to project future bad debts and put aside reserves to offset them. In a good year, a bank may increase reserves for its projected debts, thus deflating the bulge in its earnings. Major oil companies, similarly, deduct each year an amount representing depletion of petroleum reserves. Those reserves, since they are in the ground, are really an unknown quantity. And the number of barrels on the balance sheet is simply an estimate, albeit an estimate buttressed by the research of a geologist or petroleum engineer.

In a very good year, an oil company may receive a geological report asserting that reserves are smaller than previously estimated. On the basis of the report, the company may reduce the estimated value of the asset—thus increasing the percentage of it depleted by the year's operations. More depletion means a bigger deduction. A bigger deduction means lower earnings. Lower earnings mean a higher P/E ratio—but not a fundamentally less valuable company.

Sometimes accounting standards themselves seem arbitrary. U.S. companies with operations outside the country, for example, must continually revalue their foreign liabilities to reflect current exchange rates. But the value of foreign *assets* does not have to be recalculated. For example, assume a U.S. company contracts a debt in Germany of 3 million deutsche marks (DM) when the U.S. dollar purchases 3 DM. At current exchange rates, the debt goes on the balance sheet as $1 million. But perhaps the next year the dollar declines in value to 2 DM. The debt now appears as $1.5 million—which decreases earnings by $500,000. Meanwhile, the value of foreign assets remains unchanged, even though their sale would yield more dollars at 2 DM per dollar than at 3 DM per dollar. This scarcely provides a good measure of the company's relative health from year to year.

These uncertainties, arising from familiar U.S. accounting standards, might make one cautious about securities analysis based on other countries' accounting systems. In 1987, for instance, analysts were concerned about the high P/E ratios in Japan. Many thought the market greatly overvalued and due for a collapse that would burst the bubble in prices around the world. The bubble did burst, all right, but not because of a collapse in Japan, whose market rebounded smartly and soon returned to its high valuation.

To try to make sense of this situation, analysts have come up with various ways to translate Japanese numbers into U.S. equivalents—trying, one might conclude, to make oranges into apples. According to one such attempt, we can simply add 20 percent to Japanese earnings estimates— 10 percent to represent earnings of subsidiaries (which, in Japan, are not consolidated with the parent company's earnings), plus 10 percent to offset faster depreciation schedules. The resulting increase in earnings brings down the P/E ratios. But is this shortcut headed in the right direction? It doesn't account for the fact that Japanese firms can transfer slow-moving inventory to subsidiaries at a value above market price. This suggests we should discount *earnings* by some reasonable amount—say 10 percent. And that would *increase* the P/E ratio.

In general, then, take the numbers in financial statements — both foreign and domestic — with a grain of salt. In some cases, you can find electronic databases, magazines, or books with figures you can use to check your P/E estimates. If possible, compare the foreign numbers with those for a similar company traded as an ADR, since a company with ADRs must file adjusted numbers with the SEC. Insofar as financial statements can be relied upon to represent reality — rather than state or company policies — they are reliable only in their own context. Keep the oranges in one basket.

Rule 4: Know the Country

This is a large order, but you can shrink it quite a bit by concentrating on the factors that move markets. Is the country highly industrialized or less developed? What tax policies directly affect investment? What is the country's attitude toward investment in general and foreign investment in particular? Be aware of recent changes in any of these areas, for such changes will have direct, though perhaps delayed, effects on markets. Let's look at each area more closely.

The difference between developed and less-developed countries is roughly analogous to the difference between the tortoise and the hare in the famous fable. Like the tortoise, the more highly developed country tends to be slow of movement, but steadier and more predictable. In the United Kingdom, the United States, and Western Europe, growth may average only 2 or 3 percent per year. (In recent years, the highest rate of GNP growth in a Common Market country has been just over 3 percent — in Italy.) Despite their many differences and disagreements, these countries form something of an economic unit, and their markets tend to move together. You can see the common patterns in figures 6–4 through 6–7 for the United States, the United Kingdom, Japan, and Germany in the 1970s. Note especially the simultaneous bottoms in 1974.

Less-Developed Countries (LDCs)

In LDCs, growth may be bounding along at annual averages of 6 to 7 percent, and this higher rate of development may be reflected in the growth of your invested capital. Because of significant differences in the economies of LDCs, however, their markets don't all move along the same growth curves. Without the diversity and richness of highly developed countries, the LDCs are often prey to the vicissitudes of particular crops or resources. Petroleum-rich countries in the Middle East, for example, will prosper when world oil prices rise and petroleum-poor countries elsewhere languish. In the fable of the hare and the tortoise, of course, the slow but steady tortoise eventually wins the race over the speedy but erratic hare. The opposite may happen in world economics: the LDCs may well catch up and surpass the established economies. Never push an analogy beyond its limits.

Nevertheless, like the hare in the fable, less-developed economies have been prone to race ahead rapidly, then fall back with equal or greater rapidity. Consider, for example, the fate of the Mexican market in 1987. According to *The Wall Street Journal,* "The October 1987 stock market crash turned Mexico's Bolsa de Valores from the fastest growing market in the world to the fastest falling market, triggering a financial panic and peso devaluation."[3] Before the crash, the Bolsa peaked at 373,216. Then it fell to a low of 47,224 in January of 1988. By mid October of 1988, it had recovered to 191,816—up almost 400 percent from the low, but still only about 50 percent of its high in the previous year. Some of this volatility translated into the value of The Mexico Fund, a closed-end investment company trading on the NYSE (see figure 6–8).

Figure 6–4. U.S., 1970s: U.S. Commerce Department data

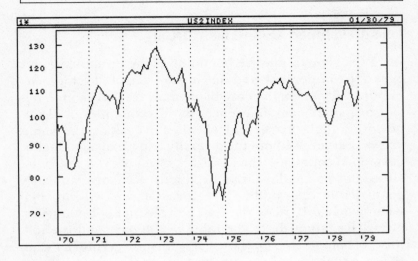

Figure 6–5. U.K., 1970s: U.S. Commerce Department data

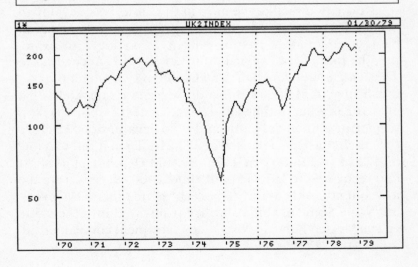

Figure 6–6. Germany, 1970s: U.S. Commerce Department data

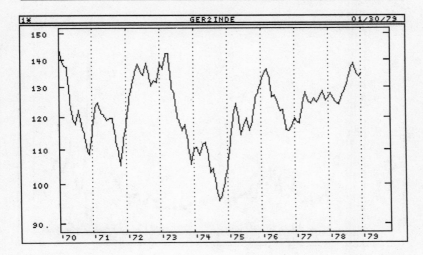

Figure 6–7. Japan, 1970s: U.S. Commerce Department data

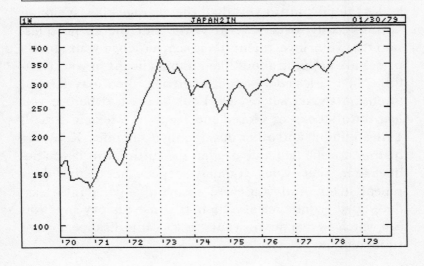

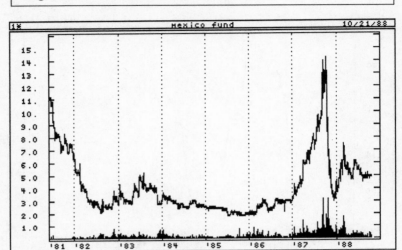

Figure 6–8. The Mexico Fund, 1981–88

Since you hold foreign stock for the long term (remember Rule 2), short-term unruliness such as Mexico's may be less important to you than the average rise (speaking optimistically) over several years. But there's no question that your investment life is scarier when your stock's prices are hopping about like jumping beans in your portfolio. In the less-developed countries, then, pay special attention to market cycles. Look backward before you leap into stocks or closed-end funds in Mexico, Brazil, Taiwan, India, and other developing economies. Knowing history doesn't help one predict the future. But if you believe in market cycles, you may suspect that history does repeat itself. And you want to avoid buying into less-developed economies at a high, because history says you can watch a great deal of your stock's value disappear quite suddenly.

Economics and Politics

One way to beat the stodginess of the slower-growing markets is to look for special situations in a country's economy. The United Kingdom, for example, was troubled for a long time by the price of the oil it imported. So the development of North Sea oil reserves gave a great boost to the U.K. economy. As an investor, you would like to get in on the beginning of such a process—after the discovery of oil (or even before, if you're prescient)—and before all the benefits of that discovery have been translated into rising stock prices. The European Community, as it moves toward 1992, should be a good place to watch for special situations. The removal of trade barriers has long-term implications for particular countries, industries, and companies. You want to find the ones affected positively, and do so early.

Tax policy can also have dramatic effects on stock values—especially when the taxes are directly related to securities transactions, as are capital gains taxes and withholding on dividends. When Austria reduced dividend withholding in the mid 1980s, investors flocked into that market. By contrast, as we noted in the previous chapter, investors bailed out of the Taipei market as rapidly as possible when Taiwan reinstituted capital gains taxes on stock appreciation in 1988.

The impact of tax change isn't always as immediate as in the previous examples. The effects of an alteration in tax policy, for example, usually don't take hold until tax-paying time the next year. This gives you the opportunity to benefit from growth over the longer term, rather than having to time your decisions more carefully than foreign investment usually allows. Incidentally, there's no reason—as the Taiwan example shows—not to look for, and look out for, relevant economic changes in LDCs. A positive change in economic situation or policy, combined with average 6 percent growth, can have a very pleasant effect on your stock's values.

Sometimes tax policy can give you a clue to another country factor you should know about: attitude toward investment, especially toward foreign investment. Is the country you're considering likely to welcome your capital with open arms? Or is it going to discourage your participation in its economy? Some countries—Austria has exemplified this attitude—look askance at investment in general. Not so long ago, stock-market investing in the United States was generally considered as respectable as riverboat gambling.

But even countries that look very favorably upon their stock markets may not be enamored of foreign investment.

Distrust of Foreign Investment

Korea and Taiwan both encourage economic growth and generally look with favor upon equity investment. But each restricts foreign equity trading to one closed-end fund. All countries are leery of having foreign investors own the bulk of a domestic company, especially if that company is defense-related or is in other ways strategic. In the United States, for example, foreign ownership of communications companies is limited to 20 percent.

The concern about foreign investment is rather a recent phenomenon—since foreign investment on any kind of scale is a recent phenomenon. In the past, most transactions with foreigners were handled privately and were relatively insignificant to the overall economy of most countries. So no one worried much about passing laws to restrict or encourage such investment. This has changed, partly because so much money has migrated into London since 1979, when the United Kingdom removed restrictions on currency exchange. Money coming into London is money going out of other countries, and these other countries have become envious. Now even the United States has to be concerned that its regulations be drawn in such a way that capital doesn't flee to other markets.

In a speech to the Securities Industry Association (SIA) in late November of 1988, for example, FRB Chairman Alan Greenspan strongly emphasized the need to keep U.S. stock markets competitive. "Inevitably," he said, "market participants will become highly sensitive to the comparative cost and efficiency of transacting in one market versus another."[4] As an international investor, you will, increasingly, find markets bidding for your dollars by improving their efficiency and economy.

For many years, French policies were motivated by a desire to protect the culture and economy from foreign influence and foreign money—and these isolating policies were compounded by nationalization of basic industries under the socialist government. Now, by contrast, France is part of the EC, indeed would like to be the leader of the EC, and has made significant movement toward free trade and competition. The French are especially concerned that restrictions against Japanese investment have diverted the flood of yen into other Europeans' economies. In the same vein, France has begun to modernize its stock-trading and clearing systems. (Clearing systems process the data generated by trades, facilitating the orderly exchange of money and security ownership.) Because the government now encourages a more favorable attitude toward foreign investment, the French market has become much more attractive to investors around the world (see figure 6–9).

Judging a country's attitude toward foreign investment is tricky. Trickier yet is correctly forecasting changes in those attitudes. Even the predispositions of one's compatriots can seem obscure and surprisingly unstable. Is the United States, for example, favorable toward foreign investment? We've described earlier the highly international flavor of our largest companies. We know that

Figure 6–9. Paris Bourse, 1985–89: CAC Index

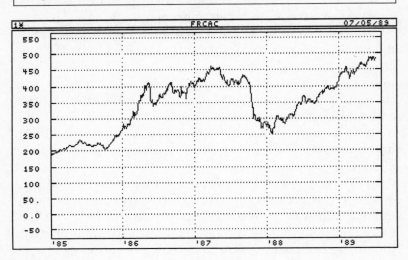

foreign investment in our national debt, especially Japanese investment, has been a significant factor in permitting government spending to remain as high as it has. Certainly the fact that NASDAQ and the NYSE list about 130 ADRs indicates that U.S. investors have substantial interest in putting their own money into other markets.

Yet there is also a great deal of uneasiness in this country about foreign ownership of corporations and real estate — enough uneasiness that the Dukakis campaign made it an issue in the 1988 elections. We clearly are nervous about handing over decisions to foreign owners — decisions that might affect labor practices and patterns of corporate charity, among other things. U.S. attitudes toward the Japanese, for example, have been, at best, mixed — combining envy, awe, and puzzlement. At worst, our economic concerns about Japan may be outright racist.

David Boaz of the Cato Institute in Washington makes that case very strongly in a *Wall Street Journal* editorial, "Yellow Peril Reinfects America." Quoting both from liberals and conservatives, Boaz illustrates a venomous undercurrent in the U.S. debate on Japan. "We've been running up the white flag," Walter Mondale declaimed in his campaign, "when we should be running up the American flag! . . . What do we want our kids to do? Sweep up around Japanese computers?"[5] Jesse Helms (R—N.C.) suggested that compensation from the U.S. government for Japanese-Americans detained in concentration camps during World War II should be linked to compensation paid by Japan to victims of Pearl Harbor—"clearly implying," Boaz writes, "[that] Japanese Americans bore some sort of racial guilt for the misdeeds of the Japanese government."[6] Boaz claims that concern about Japanese investment in the United States is far more strident and widespread than concern about, for example, British, Canadian, and Dutch investment. And it is accompanied by an increase in violence against Asians and Asian-Americans.

Despite all this hair-raising rhetoric, the United States owns vastly more in other countries—the Dow 30, as we remarked in chapter 1, have a substantial foreign presence—than other countries own here.

If such fear of foreign economic dominance can surface in U.S. politics, imagine the potential for policy change in smaller, more fragile economies. Canadian fear of U.S. influence turned the 1988 elections into a referendum on a free-trade agreement between the two neighbors. Events during the Olympic Games demonstrated, it seems clear, the latent hostility toward the United States of its allies in Korea. The Japanese, for all their involvement in foreign markets, limit foreign ownership of domestic companies, and require foreign investors to hire and compensate a Japanese voting agent. American companies are forbidden to purchase real estate in Japan—thus preventing U.S.

automakers from establishing factories there in the way that Japanese companies have established plants in the United States.[7]

Along with restrictions on foreign investment, there is a high degree of unity in the Japanese market. Moreover, a very large percentage of Japanese stock is owned by other corporations "for eternity," according to the concept of *zaibatsu*. Removing a substantial portion of stock from public buying and selling pressures means the marketplace can become rather isolated from reality, from fundamentals. The market, therefore, is easily managed—as if it were a team of players with unified goals. If sentiment is bullish, for example, investors don't want to violate team spirit, and perhaps lose face, by selling their stocks. Exactly this kind of teamwork may, in fact, be contributing to those current high P/E ratios that make some analysts so nervous.[8]

To reiterate: part of knowing a country is knowing its attitude toward investment and toward foreign investors. And there's no denying that you're in a tricky psychological area here, since attitudes are about as stable as quicksand. Attitudes, and the policies that make them effective, are subject to change; and those changes can mean substantial movement in markets.

The cautious investor tries to take a longer-term view. Attitudes may look very favorable at the moment in a particular country, but perhaps that country has a long history of being negative toward investment, or a history of rapid change in attitude. Sometimes a highly positive attitude is linked with unusually high prices and volume of trade— which may well indicate a speculative bubble ready to burst. Conversely, a negative attitude, seen against a more favorable historical position, may be just a temporary phenomenon, a fit of national pique that will quickly pass—and, therefore, a signal to the contrarian to get in and profit from the coming return to normality. In general, however, you want to avoid sending your dollars where they aren't wanted.

Rule 5: Know Yourself

This is just as important as knowing the company and the country. If you are an experienced investor, chances are good that you buy and sell according to a system of some sort—partly conscious, partly second nature. Whatever works for you, naturally, is good: and a great variety of methods do, in fact, work.

Some investors stress fundamentals, some are more technically oriented, and many combine the two types of analysis. Fundamentalists watch the numbers discussed in this chapter, looking for signs that a company is healthy and poised to prosper in its market. They won't be overly nervous about buying a stock they can't follow in a U.S. daily paper and will be content to check the price occasionally in a foreign source.

Investors inclined toward technical analysis, by contrast, place special emphasis on market data, and like to watch daily and monthly price movements. Some investors wouldn't read an annual report on a bet; some insist on reading every word published by companies they own—and won't buy a company whose reports are unavailable or available only in a foreign language.

Some investors buy only blue chip stocks, and others specialize in smaller companies.

These choices are personal, and they are all workable. Just know what makes you comfortable, and don't violate your established method when you start buying foreign stock. A recommended security may be just fine for the person recommending it—but not for you; so stay away from it. Be patient. If you like small-cap companies, don't get into a global monster just because someone else thinks it's hot. If you're comfortable with blue chips, on the other hand, don't start buying small companies that fit some available niche in Australia just because you want foreign diversification. If you savor each word in the annual reports of all your companies, don't buy a company that's going to send you literature in a language in which you can't say "liabilities." (You might be able to find an attractive, similar company trading as an ADR.)

Summary

All things (even rules of investment) are subject to change — and it didn't take Black Monday to teach us that. Change drives markets; change is adventure. One such change is the growing desire among Americans to look outward into global markets, not just for profits but for contact with other cultures. The peaceful, respectful entry of U.S. investors into other markets (and the reciprocal entry of other nations' investors into our own) has the feeling of adventure about it, the feeling of change for the better. To risk one's money on the enterprise and creativity of men and women doing business in other countries is to pay tribute both to them and to ourselves.

There's a world of opportunities out there — quite literally. Look for the one that's right for you. If you use the five rules to screen a recommendation (or a hunch of your own, for that matter), and the stock in question doesn't subject you to one of the pitfalls we've described, buy it. And hold it. But while you hold it, keep questioning your own rules. If it's necessary to know yourself, your company, and your country before investing, then it's equally necessary to keep that knowledge up to date during the holding period.

In the spirit of continuous questioning and suiting your methods to your world view, the next chapter explores another way to select a foreign stock — a technician's, rather than a fundamentalist's approach. In fact, the two opposing views can work together quite comfortably in helping you select your own investments.

Endnotes

1. This is rather a long, though intriguing, story that is neither entirely complete nor without its controversial elements. More details are available, among other places, in Randall W. Forsyth's "Quiet Culprits," *Barron's*, October 17, 1988, and in David McClain's book, *Apocalypse on Wall Street*, (Homewood, Ill.: Dow Jones-Irwin, 1988).

2. Tim Metz, *Black Monday* (New York: William Morrow, 1988), p. 251.

3. See Matt Moffett, "Mexico's Market at Only Half of Pre-Crash Peak, Remains Lethargic, Reflecting Persistent Doubts," *The Wall Street Journal*, October 24, 1988, p. C10.

4. *Investor's Daily*, December 1, 1988.

5. David Boaz, "Yellow Peril Reinfects America," *The Wall Street Journal*, April 7, 1989. [Ellipsis in original.]

6. *Ibid.*

7. *Ibid.*

8. See, for example, an interview with Paul Tudor Jones, *Barron's*, October 17, 1988, p. 16.

CHAPTER 7

Charting Your Course: Technical Analysis

Technical analysts look beyond a company's fiscal vital signs to concentrate on the market itself — comparing current stock-price trends and volume to past patterns, for example. There are, for the technician, patterns in human affairs — business cycles, for example — and such patterns can be discerned by studying the charts that record stock-price movements. A strict technician, as technical analysts are called, might operate with nothing more than the data derived from such charts, never consulting the company's balance sheet or considering the country's leadership. Theoretically, at least, the technician believes that future price movements can (within some range of probability) be predicted by looking at past prices.

Though we wouldn't advocate taking a purely technical approach, the fact is that finding technical data about foreign markets will sometimes be easier than locating good information about a particular company. You have to use what you can get. Besides, your stock is going to have difficulty moving up if the market is going down, a fact that argues for knowing as much about the market as you can. So this chapter should be seen as complementary to chapter 6, not contradictory. Consider your potential foreign investments from both the fundamental and technical perspectives. There's wisdom in each.

How Technical Is Technical Analysis?

For most investors, technical analysis probably seems too, well, technical. How can one hope to compete with full-time professionals whose analytical tools, background knowledge, and resources are far beyond the average investor's? In fact, one can't, any more than one can compete with doctors in diagnosing diseases and prescribing medicine. But one doesn't need a medical degree to know it's unhealthy to overeat, smoke, or drink too much. Nor does one need to understand "bullish reversals" or "head-and-shoulders patterns" to tell whether a stock's price is moving up or down on a chart. A little basic knowledge can go a long way in helping us maintain our financial—as well as our personal—well-being. Sometimes all you need is enough understanding to recognize a questionable recommendation, whether it's a doctor's prescription or a broker's tout. Asking for a second opinion is permissible for investors as well as for patients.

A more serious reservation about technical analysis is that it focuses on the short term. Most technicians are looking for gains within four to six weeks. And we've said that successful foreign investment is by nature a long-term game. What we're borrowing from the technicians, however, stays pretty close to common sense. We don't mean to encourage you to speculate short term against professional traders.

It helps to remember, though, that even the professionals are sometimes wrong. Dead wrong. Disastrously wrong. You don't have to be right every time, and you can't expect to be. No matter what method you use, no matter how mathematically complex your calculations and thorough your data, your success depends on what happens in the future. And the future is uncharted territory. As we said in the previous chapter, investment is an adventure. Every time you buy or sell a stock, you take a risk. Doing a bit of analysis first helps you reduce that risk to whatever level you find tolerable.

A Technician's View of Japan

Technicians are also called chartists, because charts are so important to their work. So let's look at some charts to see what's significant about them. It is, incidentally, much easier, and much cheaper to find charts of foreign markets—they're in *Barron's* and *Investor's Daily*—than to find charts for particular companies. For the most part, then, you'll be looking at charts for the market you're thinking of entering—charts like figure 7–1 representing Japan, for example. Analyzing the chart for a market is no different from analyzing a stock chart.

At first glance, you might say simply that the Japanese market goes up. Spectacularly and continuously. On the whole, it does. Starting from under 200 in early 1969, it rises to its all-time high of 2,000 by early 1988—better than a tenfold increase. Since this is a book about long-term international investing, we could smile smugly here and extol the virtures of buying and holding in such a splendid market. But a skeptic might ask, with a malicious gleam in his or her eye, how would one have known in 1968 that this marvelous ascent was about to take place? Or, the skeptic might object, let's say one discovered the market at some other date—such as 1973 or 1975 or late 1988.

157

Figure 7–1. Japan, 1969–88: U.S. Commerce Department data

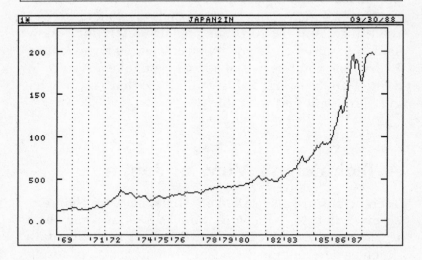

Figure 7–2. Japan, 1973–74: U.S. Commerce Department data

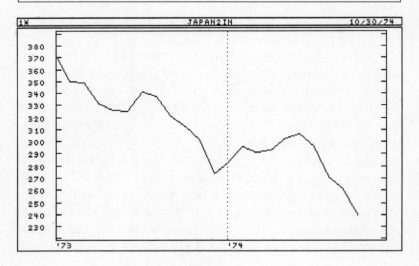

Forceful objections, these. If we take a closer view of certain sections of the chart, we find periods of significant decline. Look more closely at 1973 and 1974 in figure 7–2. Starting from a peak of about 370 in January of 1973, the market drops all year—except for a modest trip upward in the summer—until it has fallen almost 100 points by December. In early 1974, prices move up, reaching a high of a little over 300 by early June. But then the slide resumes, steadily and steeply, until the market hits a low of 240 at the end of September. That's a loss of more than 35 percent during less than two years. And 1975 was even more heartrending. The chart in figure 7–3 begins on a fairly steep upgrade, and by late April the index for the Japanese market is up near 300. The patient investor who bought back in early 1973 is probably overjoyed. Summertime is coming and the market is up more than 50 points from its low of the previous winter. Then the chart goes up over the crest of the hill and plummets to 270 by the time the kids go back to school. Worse, as you can see from looking back at the long-term chart, repeated as figure 7–4, the market doesn't surpass its 1973 high point of 370 until 1978. That's over five years of waiting for one's investment to pay off.

It takes a great deal of patience to maintain faith in a market for such an extended period. Even in 1987 owners of Japanese stocks had to suffer through a long downturn. From early June to September, as you can see in figure 7–5, the index tumbled from above 1950 to 1650—losing 16 percent in little more than half a year. As we said in chapter 6, experienced investors generally have a consistent approach of one sort or another. Not everyone would pick the same points to get into Japanese stocks. So we'll look closely at three different methods of using charts to screen stocks. But first we need to do a brief exercise in chart reading. For not all charts are created equal, and you can be quite misled if you compare different types of charts.

Figure 7–3. Japan, 1975: U.S. Commerce Department data

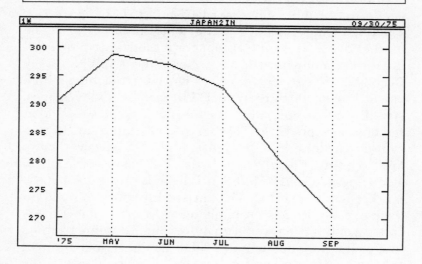

Figure 7–4. Japan, 1969–88: U.S. Commerce Department data

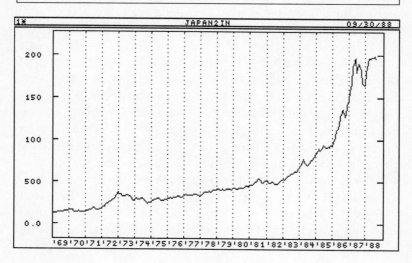

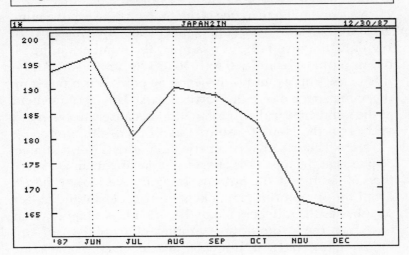

Figure 7-5. Japan, 1987: U.S. Commerce Department data

Reading the Charts

Always check first to see where a chart begins. In figure
7–5, for instance, the vertical axis starts at 1600 points.
Look at the chart again, and imagine how it would appear
if the numbers on the left hand side ran all the way down
to zero. Visualize the long blank space at the bottom before you get to the line representing the movement of the
market. Cutting off the bottom like this greatly magnifies
gains and losses. If you assumed that figure 7–5 began at
zero, for example, instead of at 1600, you would think it
depicted a much greater loss than 16 percent—in fact, it
would look like about an 85 percent drop. (If the vertical
intervals were each equal to 1, the value would fall from
over 7 to about 1.) Imagine the chart as a picture of an

airplane's flight: if you thought the bottom represented the ground, you'd believe a crash was imminent.

A second thing to notice is the spacing between the numbers. In figures 7–1 through 7–5, vertical spacings are all regular. In figure 7–5, for example, the numbers jump 50 points a time—from 1600 to 1650 to 1700 and so on. And—this is the important point—each 50-point jump takes up the same space along the vertical axis. This arrangement of the numbers is called arithmetic—because you can mark spaces on the chart by simple addition of 50 points.

Not all charts are arithmetic. Sometimes, for instance, 50 points at the top of the chart will take up much less space than 50 points at the bottom. Imagine the look of figure 7–5 if the 50-point intervals kept getting closer and closer together as the numbers along the left side got higher. That is, in fact, the layout of the "semilog" chart of figure 7–6A. Below it, for contrast, is an arithmetic chart for the same period (1947 to 1988). Note that the charts start at zero, and the semilog chart uses 500-point intervals instead of 50-point gaps. You can clearly see that 500 points at the top occupies much less space than 500 points at the bottom. These charts are called "semilog" because the sequence of numbers on the vertical scale is logarithmic rather than arithmetic. If the mathematical terms leave you cold (one of the authors isn't overly fond of numbers either), think of the charts as the equal-space (arithmetic) and unequal-space (semilog) types. For, as you can see from the following semilog chart, there's a great deal more space between 0 and 500 than there is between 1,500 and 2,000—even though both represent intervals of 500 points. And notice how the semilog chart flattens out that wonderfully steep slope the arithmetic chart shows for the 1980s!

Now you're probably wondering why anyone would want to level out that lovely, vertiginous ascent? Such a picture is a marvelous stock-marketing tool, after all (to take a brokerish point of view). Who could look at that

Figure 7–6A. Japan, 1947–88: Semilog chart

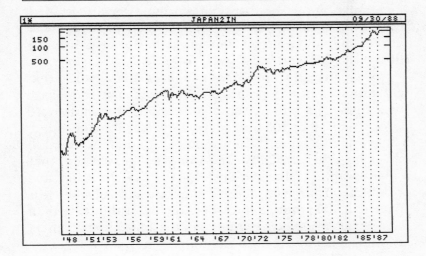

Figure 7–6B. Japan, 1947–88: Arithmetic chart

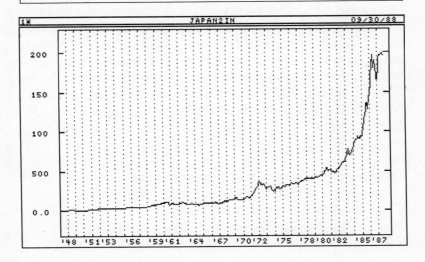

Himalayan illustration and not want to have it mirrored by his or her brokerage balance? Moreover, that tantalizing picture on the equal-spaced, arithmetic graph is absolutely true: it shows exactly what happened in the Japanese market, 50-point gain by 50-point gain. But does it really illustrate what you most want to know?

As an investor, you aren't looking for a stock that will gain another 50 points on the index. You're looking for a stock that will increase your capital by another 10 percent—or 50 or 100 percent or whatever. In your mind, a 50-point gain from 1,950 to 2,000 is not, in fact, equal to a 50-point gain from 200 to 250. One is a tiny step, the other a giant leap. And the semilog chart is keyed to that sort of thinking. That's why figure 7–6A, for example, allots less space to a 500-point gain toward the top of the scale than it does for a 500-point gain near the bottom. The chart accounts, visually, for the fact that turning 100 dollars (or yen) into 500 is a great deal more significant than turning 1,000 into 1,500.

Notice something else about the chart—something a little less obvious than the differing spaces granted to 500-point leaps. On the semilog chart, spaces are in fact divided in a regular way: the space between 500 and 1,000, for example, equals the space between 1,000 and 2,000. And if the chart went up twice as high (in numbers), it would allow just the same amount of space to the jump from 2,000 to 4,000 points. Every time the index doubles, in other words, you move the same distance up the side of the chart. The leap from 500 to 1,000 is the same distance on the chart as the leap from 1,000 to 2,000 and so on. In this way, the semilog graph gives you a better visual image than the arithmetic chart of how often you could have doubled your money in the Japanese market between 1944 and 1988.

And if that seems like rather a long story, it has a short moral: apples to apples, oranges to oranges. When you're comparing markets (or individual stocks), make sure you are looking at charts of the same type, for arithmetic and semilog charts give you very different pictures of the same investment events.

Using the Charts

Buy low; sell high. What could be simpler? One of the problems with stocks, of course, is that you have no control over the price. If you're dealing in used cars or other tangible items that you can sell yourself, and you have the gift of gab, you may be able to influence the buying and selling prices. When you're purchasing the item, you shrewdly locate its weak points and use them against the seller—all the while keeping quiet about those attractive features that you will exploit when you sell the car for a higher price. Perhaps you're handy and you can fix the car up a little to increase its value. With stocks, on the other hand, you pay or receive the quoted price and that's that. There's no legitimate way you can influence the market to like the stock you own and want to sell high. You have to guess at the psychology of buyer and seller. And that is part of what you're doing when you look at the charts; you're taking a reading of the market's temperature, getting a sense of whether it's about to heat up or cool down.

In the balance of this chapter, we're going to describe three patterns to look for on charts when you're checking out a stock. None of the three methods is infallible. All are long-term. Here they are: you want to buy when the market is depressed and quiet, just starting to move up, or already on an upward trend.

Buy when the market is:

1. Depressed and quiet
2. Just starting up
3. On an uptrend

Which method you pick will depend upon your selection system and your patience. We'll look at examples of each, beginning with buying when the market is depressed and quiet—or "in the doldrums."

In the Doldrums

A quiet market? Actually, markets are always moving, which is why we read about daily highs and lows, weekly highs and lows, 52-week highs and lows, and so on. But sometimes prices seem to be trapped for days, weeks, months, or even years between a particular high point and a particular low point. The market may hit each of these highs and lows more than once, but seem unable to break through either of them to go on to new highs or lows. These flat spots—the doldrums, metaphorically—offer great potential rewards for investors. When the market does finally break out, it sometimes surges up dramatically— almost as if it had been gathering energy for a leap. And, if you were to visit the country during that quiet period, you might see evidence of that energy in shopping patterns, traffic jams at rush hour, heavy construction activity, or other signs of economic health. Take a look at figure 7-7, a chart for the Canadian market during the middle 1970s, for example. From early 1975 to early 1978, the Canadian market goes up a ways and comes back down a ways. But it can't get above 120 or below 105. It has hit the doldrums, after rebounding from the low point reached during the recession in 1974. (See figure 7-8.) Those who bought Canadian stocks during the quiet years of 1975, 1976, and 1977 had to wait patiently for a few years while the market bobbed up and down in essentially calm waters. But they were rewarded by a bull market that began in 1978 and took prices up to 400 in 1987—despite losses during the recession of 1980 to 1982 when Canada, along with other

Figure 7–7. Canada, 1975–78: U.S. Commerce Department data

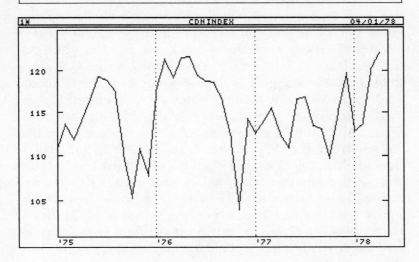

Figure 7–8. Canada, 1974–78: U.S. Commerce Department data

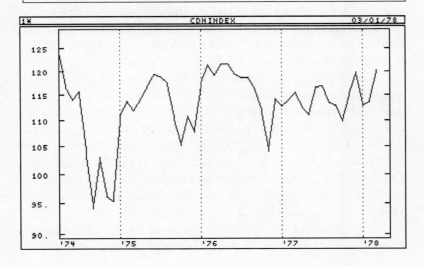

Western markets, was in a slump. (See figure 7–9.) The reward was worth the wait.

What was going on south of Canada's border during these years? As you can tell from figures 7–10 and 7–11, Western markets sometimes track one another—but not always. During the slump of the mid 1970s, the U.S. market was just as sluggish as the Canadian. But when Canada took off in 1977, the United States stayed behind. Figure 7–10 is a picture of a market in the doldrums—for four years! After rebounding with substantial vigor from the 1974 bottom, the U.S. market peaks in 1976 at 115, drifts down below 100 in early 1978, climbs almost to 115 later that year, drops again below 105, then climbs slowly during 1979 and finally tops 115 late in the year. In 1980, as figure 7–11 shows, the market breaks out of its slump— with the energy built up during those long years of relative inactivity. But late in 1980 it collapses again until 1982. When the U.S. market comes to life in August of 1982, it does so with a newborn's burst of energy, rising from about 125 in August of 1982 to just over 350 before the crash in 1987. (See figure 7.39.) That's a gain of about 225 percent during the legendary bull run of the 1980s. (If you're wondering about the numbers, we're using the Standard and Poor's Corporation (S&P) index here, not the DJIA, which, of course, peaked over 2,700 in 1987).

Like the United States, Canada (figure 7.12) enjoyed a stock-market surge in the early 1980s followed by a decline that had wiped out a substantial portion of those gains by 1982. And in 1982 the market in Canada took off toward the late 1987 peak—just like the U.S. market, as you can see from figure 7–13, a chart for the Toronto Stock Exchange (TSE). (Note that the numbers are different— because we're using a different Canadian index—but the upward movement is the same for all indexes.)

The chart shows that the Toronto market rose from about 1,400 at the low in 1982 to a high of just over 4,000

Figure 7–9. Canada, 1978–88: U.S. Commerce Department data

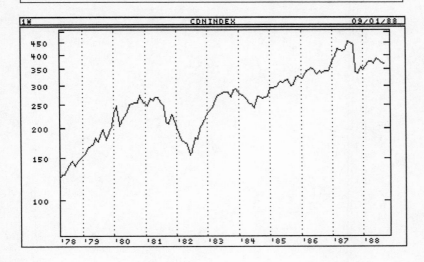

Figure 7–10. U.S., 1974–79: S&P 500 Index

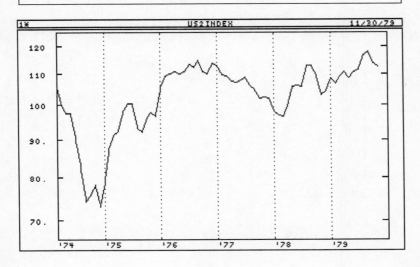

Figure 7–11. U.S., 1979–82: S&P 500 Index

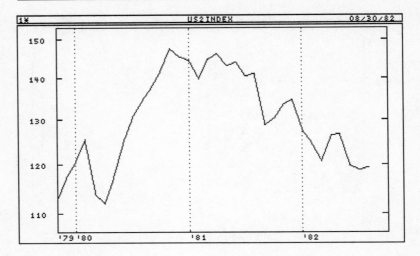

Figure 7–12. Canada, 1978–82: U.S. Commerce Department data

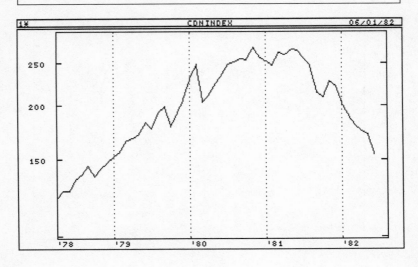

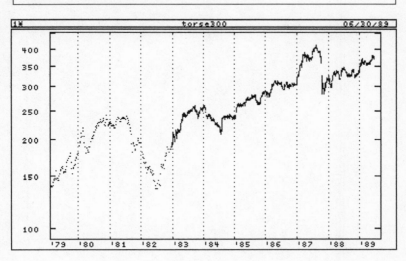

Figure 7–13. Canada, 1979–89: TSE 300

in 1988. That's a gain of better than 180 percent. The pattern, then, is the same for Canada and the United States—long years in the doldrums followed by a surge of energy. Only the timing is different. Investing in the United States, with that long, slow period in the 1970s and early 1980s, required more patience than investing in Canada.

As you can see from figures 7–14 and 7–15, the United States and Canada have continued along somewhat similar paths since the crash. Somewhat similar, but not the same.

By late 1988, both Canada and the United States had bounced back somewhat from the bottom reached in 1987 (late October for Canada, late December for the United States). In Toronto, the market recovered close to half its loss by June of 1988: after falling from above 400 to about 290, it gained back about 60 points before backing off. In the United States, however, the market recovered less than

Figure 7–14. Canada, 1986–88: TSE 300

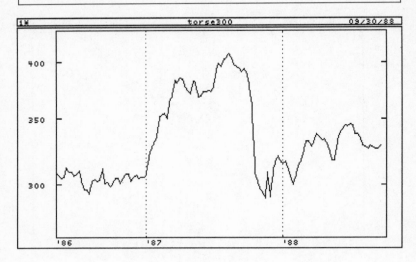

Figure 7–15. U.S., 1986–88: S&P 500 Index

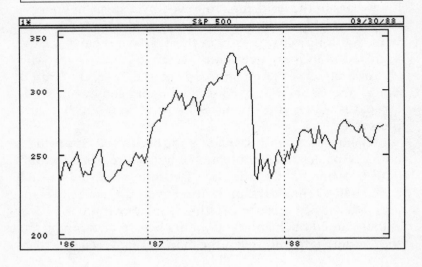

one-third of its losses by June. After having fallen from almost 340 to below 240, it moved up to about 260—and then dropped off. Although the overall pictures are similar, the percentages are quite different—at least for the short term. The more interesting question is whether the markets have hit the doldrums once more, and whether they will continue the upward surge of the 1980s or drop again.

Other Markets

How were other developed markets faring during the past decades? Figure 7–16, a chart of a German index for the years from 1961 to 1983, provides another example of the long, quiet spell in the West. From 1961 through 1982—more than a decade—the market seemed trapped between 155 and 85. It was especially quiet between 1974 and 1982—unable to break out of a groove between about 115 and 140.

In Germany itself, short-term investors with access to continuous information had the chance to make money: the difference between 85 and 155, after all, is substantial. Even the gap between 115 and 140 leaves room for some profit (or loss). But long-term investors had quite a wait for the bull market of 1982. When the bull market did arrive, however, it was spectacular—as you can see at the far right of figure 7–16. From under 115 in 1982 the market surged up to 340 by 1986, a gain of almost 200 percent. Figure 7–17 shows the continuation of this happy story, from 1983 to early 1986. Unlike the United States and Canadian markets, however, the German stock market peaked in 1986 instead of continuing to advance to new highs in 1987. When October of 1987 hit the German market, it had been in the doldrums for over a year—which shows, unfortunately, that up is not the only way out of a quiet period in the marketplace. You can go rushing down out of the doldrums, too.

Figure 7–16. Germany, 1961–83: U.S. Commerce Department data

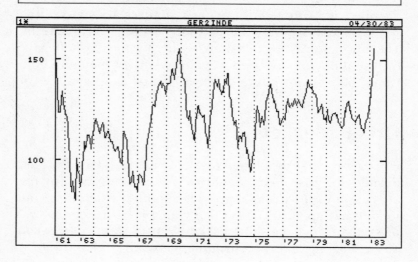

Figure 7–17. Germany, 1983–88: U.S. Commerce Department data

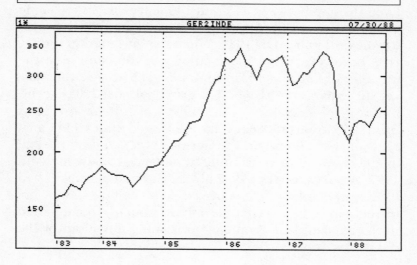

Italy

Now for the negative examples. You can enter a quiet market, wait patiently for months or years, and get clobbered. Italy in the 1960s and 1970s provides a classic example of that. After sliding precipitously downhill during the first half of the 1960s, the Italian market became boring for the latter half of the decade.

As you can see, after tumbling from 190 down to 95, the market went to sleep—tossing fitfully between 95 and 120 (see figure 7–19). Sometime during this period, you might have decided that Italy was a prime example of the "depressed and quiet" market that has such potential for the foreign investor. You would have bought Italian stocks, waited patiently, and, in 1970 and 1971, the events shown in figure 7–20 would have happened to you. Instead of breaking out at the top, the Milan market crashed through the bottom—past 95 down to 75.

Surely, you're thinking, this is the place to buy—at 75 when the market has bottomed out. The next movement is, in fact, sharply upward, to 125 in 1973. Far from recovering, however, the market falls from there to a new bottom below 75 in 1975. (See figure 7–21.)

Now have we reached a good point to invest? Trying to "fish the bottom"—catching stocks right at, or just after, the nadir of a downward plunge—is tricky. What information assures that a compensating rise in price lies ahead? Reliable information is not, after all, the hallmark of foreign markets. International markets are chancy enough without adding risk. After apparently hitting rock-bottom in 1975, Italy didn't become a bull market. By the end of the decade it had leveled out around 60. (See figure 7–22—and here we shift to a new index.)

Finally, in 1980, the Milan market breaks out of the top of its range, doubling in value from the low 60s to about 135. But, as you can see in figure 7–23, this is not an early beginning to the bull market of the 1980s.

Figure 7–18. Italy, 1960–65: U.S. Commerce Department data

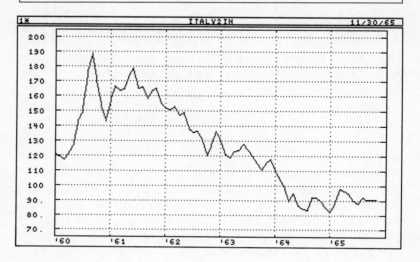

Figure 7–19. Italy, 1966–70: U.S. Commerce Department data

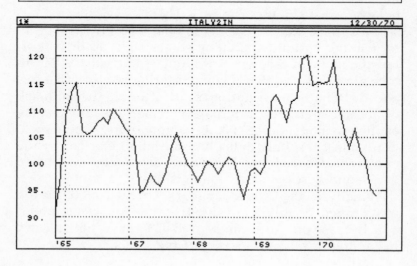

Figure 7–20. Italy, 1970–71: U.S. Commerce Department data

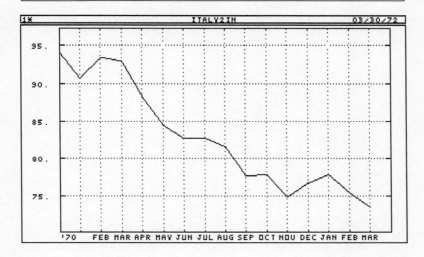

Figure 7–21. Italy, 1965–75: U.S. Commerce Department data

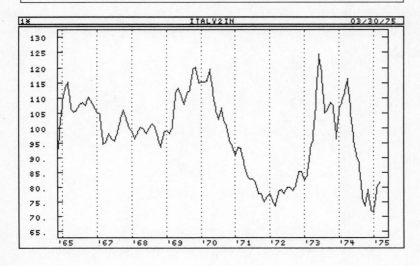

Figure 7–22. Italy, 1978–80: U.S. Commerce Department data

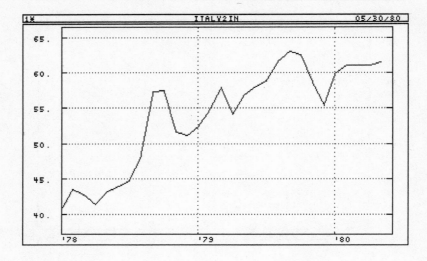

Figure 7–23. Italy, 1980–84: U.S. Commerce Department data

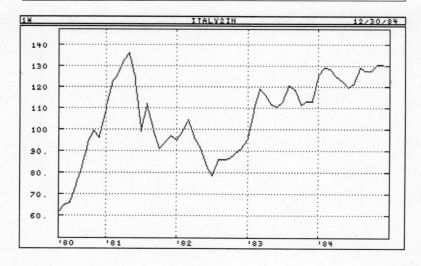

Like Canada, the United States, and Germany, Italy experiences a downturn that bottoms out in 1982. The patient investor must wait four years for the market to top the peak it reached in 1981. And, as you can see, 1983 and 1984 are pretty quiet years on the Italian bourse. At this point, the international investor might well be excused for losing patience with Italy and buying stock somewhere — anywhere — else. Alas, this loss of patience would take the investor out of the market just before one of the more spectacular bull markets in the developed world — a 340 percent gain from 130 in late 1984 to 575 in 1986. (See figure 7–24.) Of course the investor who regains faith in the Italian market in 1986 suffers the same fate as the investor who buys into Germany at the same time. Instead of taking off with the United States and Canadian markets in 1986 and 1987, the Italian market just dwindles away until early in 1988.

We never said it would be easy.

Catching a Wave

Those with somewhat less patience might be asking if there isn't a way to avoid spending years waiting for a market to turn around. Without exactly requiring instant gratification, most of us enjoy savoring our successes sooner rather than later — by looking in *Barron's* a couple of weeks after investing, for example, or even a couple of months, and counting our gains. A pleasant way to do this is to find a market that has been quiet and now is ready to move up. This, too, takes patience, but of a different sort. Instead of putting your money into a quiet market and waiting for the action to resume, you wait for the market to get moving and then buy just in time to catch the new wave of prosperity. Let's look again at Japan during the 1970s and 1980s, repeated once more as figure 7–25.

Figure 7–24. Italy, 1984–88: U.S. Commerce Department data

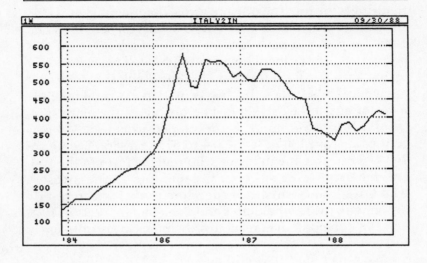

Figure 7–25. Japan, 1969–88: U.S. Commerce Department data

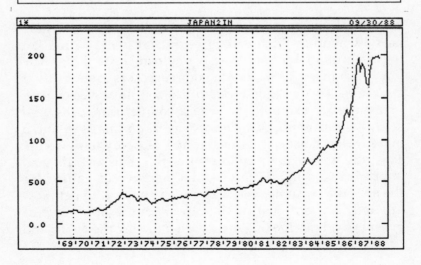

From a long-term perspective, this market is very quiet during the years from 1972 through 1978. The time to buy, then, is the spring of 1978, when the market finally breaks through the previous high reached in 1972. Instead of getting in during the doldrums and waiting patiently for the next wave, you sit out the doldrums on the sidelines and buy shortly after the market breaks out at the top.

What happened after the market broke through 370? Look at figure 7–26. The market went up almost without interruption for the next year. After peaking at 415 (about a 12 percent gain over 370), it hit the doldrums again for most of 1979. Then it ran up once more from a low of 405 in 1979 to a high of almost 450 in 1980—a bit better than a 10 percent gain in about a year. But this turns out not to be the beginning of something big—just the prelude to another flat spot in the early 1980s. After that, however, comes the miracle of the 1980s. The real takeoff point, as figure 7–27 shows, turns out to be in late 1982—in Japan as in the United States, Canada, and Europe.

While we're back in Japan, let's use its market to illustrate the relativity of terms like *quiet* and *doldrums*. What looks like a flat spot on the long-term chart can be quite choppy seen in close focus. Look, for example, at figure 7–28, a semilog chart for Japan from 1947 to 1989. Notice how unexciting the 1960s appear on this chart.

As a long-term investor, who could get interested in Japanese stocks during these years? For the speculator, however, this was a volatile market with substantial opportunity for gain and loss. Don't believe it? Take a look at figure 7–29, a close-up of the years from 1959 through 1968.

If you had gotten into this market in January of 1960 and out in mid 1961, you would have seen your money grow by 45 percent, more or less—from about 77 to about 112. And in just a few weeks during 1961 you would have seen your money depleted by about 38 percent when the market fell from 112 to 70. Boring or breathtaking? It all depends

Figure 7–26. Japan, 1978–80: U.S. Commerce Department data

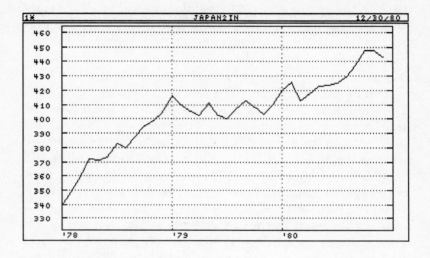

Figure 7–27. Japan, 1980–88: U.S. Commerce Department data

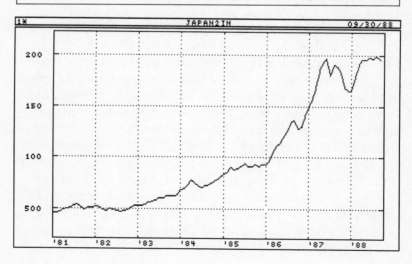

Figure 7–28.   Japan, 1947–88: U.S. Commerce Department data

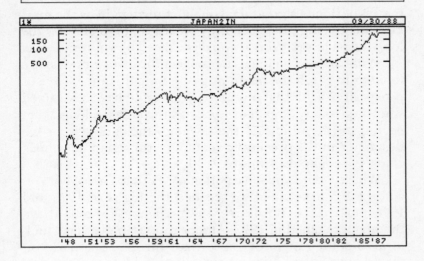

Figure 7–29.   Japan, 1959–68: U.S. Commerce Department data

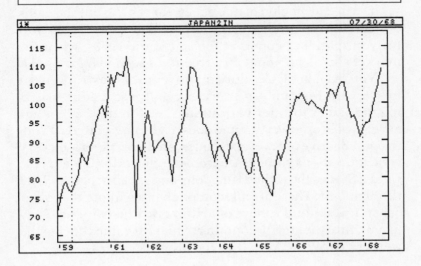

on your perspective—which, for present purposes, is long-term. When you buy and hold for a period of years, you may experience a great deal of short-term pain as the market sails through those choppy places that look flat on the long-term charts. Your reward is earned by your patience.

What about Canada as a prospect for investors who are looking to catch the beginning of a long-distance wave of prosperity? With that objective, you would have restrained your urge to buy Canadian stocks all through the long, quiet period in the middle of the decade—those doldrums we described in the preceding section of this chapter, whose chart is repeated as figure 7–30.

Where would you have gotten in? Perhaps in early 1978, when the market finally exceeded the highs of 1975 and 1976; perhaps not until early 1979, when prices rose above the highs reached in 1973. At any rate, Canada was stuck in a 20-point range for more than three years, and you would have been well justified in withholding your investment capital during that time. For that matter, you would have done well to stay out of the Canadian market through almost all of the 1970s—see figure 7–31.

The decade included one good year—1972; but the gains of that year were more than obliterated in 1974. The reward for your patience comes at the end of the 1970s, when the market shoots up about 60 percent, as seen in figure 7–32.

You may, in fact, endure many years of frustration as a long-term investor if you aren't especially successful at picking the places to enter various markets. In this as in other aspects of life, however, time does heal some wounds. From the perspective of several decades, stock markets look very good indeed—as you can see from the charts for Canada, the United States, the United Kingdom, and Japan in figures 7–33 through 7–36. These are all semilog charts without the roller-coaster peaks and valleys of arithmetic illustrations. They just picture the steady doubling of market values during the years from World War II to the present.

184

Figure 7–30. Canada, 1974–78: U.S. Commerce Department data

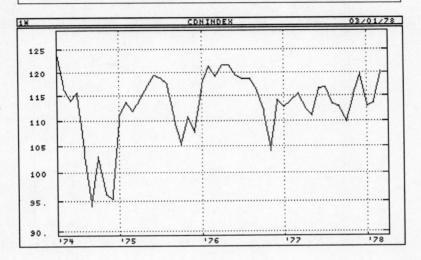

Figure 7–31. Canada, 1970–78: U.S. Commerce Department data

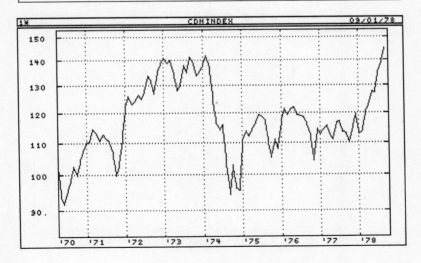

185

Figure 7–32. Canada, 1978–81: U.S. Commerce Department data

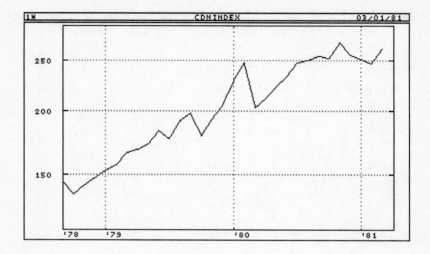

Figure 7–33. Canada, 1947–88: U.S. Commerce Department data

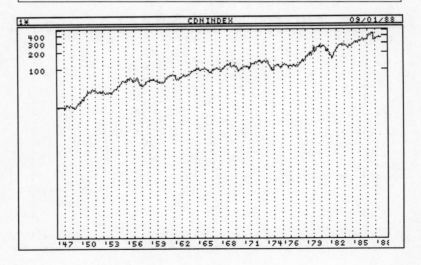

Figure 7–34. U.S., 1945–88: U.S. Commerce Department data

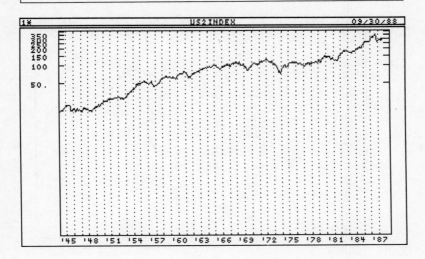

Figure 7–35. U.K., 1945–88: U.S. Commerce Department data

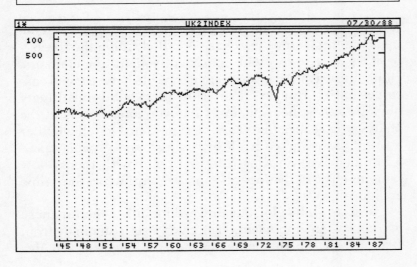

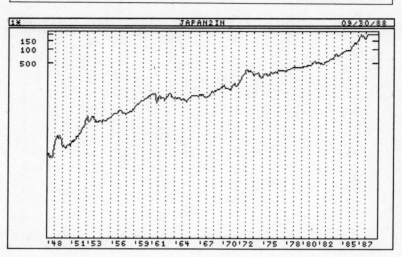

Figure 7–36. Japan, 1948–88: U.S. Commerce Department data

Riding the Trend

A third and somewhat shorter-term technique for screening a potential stock purchase is called riding the trend — or, if we were to stay with consistently nautical metaphors, riding the wave. An investment cliché fits here: a trend continues until it reverses itself. Now that sounds insultingly obvious at first hearing, but when you look closely at the charts, you realize that it's sometimes hard to tell whether a trend has reversed itself or has just, so to speak, taken a holiday. We can illustrate this point with the by-now familiar chart of the Japanese market, repeated a third time as figure 7–37.

Despite all its glorious upward mobility, the Japanese market has quiet moments. The chart rises stunningly from 1970 to 1972, starting under 150 and peaking near 400. But

Figure 7–37.   Japan, 1948–88: U.S. Commerce Department data

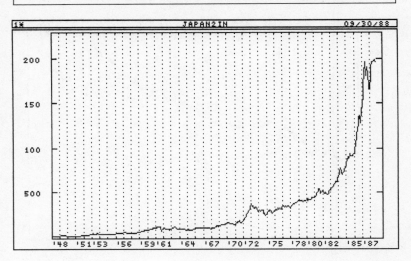

the trend line flattens in the fall of 1972. Not until 1978 does the market finally reach 400, and the real takeoff doesn't begin until the next decade. That's a long, painful hiatus for the investor—even though, in the very long term, the upward trend seems continuous. Even the smaller hesitation in 1981 and 1982, when the market stalled around 500, could have been a rather trying time for investors.

Australia provides another good example of the difficulties of riding a trend. Look at figure 7–38, a chart of the Australian market in the 1980s.

From 1982 to Black Monday in October of 1987, the overall trend in Australia is up—and most of us would be quite happy to have ridden it during those years. We would have endured some frustration at the beginning, when the market stalled around 500, and again in 1984, when the trend line flattens out between 500 and 1,000. But over the course of these years the index climbs from below 500

Figure 7–38. Australia, 1982–88: All Ordinaries

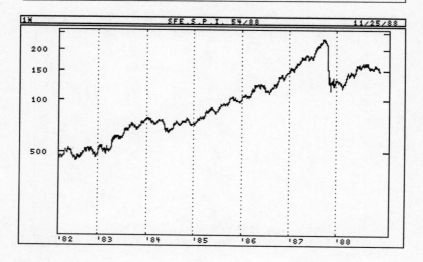

Figure 7–39. U.S., 1982–88: U.S. Commerce Department data

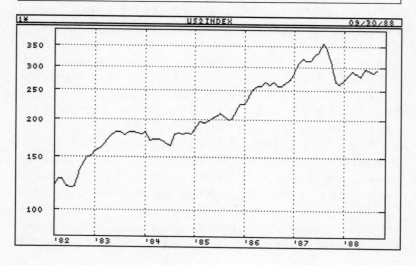

to over 2,000—before slipping backward after the crash. But that's well over a 300 percent gain. Compare that to figure 7–39, a chart of the U.S. market during the same period.

Although the trend is up here, too (with significant interruptions), the gain up to October of 1987 is around 200 percent. Australia looks pretty good by contrast.

Summary

Why look at country charts? After all, you're investing in companies, not countries—unless you're buying one of the two-dozen or so country funds we discussed in chapter 2. The charts are simply another useful way of screening your investment. A company—a fund, for that matter—is going to have great difficulty increasing in value in a falling market. And the charts help you judge whether the market is more likely to charge ahead or slide back after you make your investment.

Why not look at company charts? The patterns are the same. Stocks, like markets, establish trends and stay in them until they reverse themselves. They slide into the doldrums and stay there until something triggers a movement above or below their established limits. Unfortunately, such charts are even harder to come by than country charts. For many stocks that strike your fancy, they simply won't be available anywhere. When you're following an investment, you should consider making your own chart, plotting the weekly highs and lows if they are available. Even monthly information helps. If you have a computer, keep your eyes open for affordable quotation services that match your portfolio. It is possible now, though it is fairly expensive, to monitor many stocks and, with the proper software, to print out charts based on their price history.

As time passes, the information we need to make informed investment decisions in global markets can only become more readily available. In fact, accessibility of index charts took a leap forward between drafts of this book. (See appendix 5 for currently available services.) In this, as in all phases of international investing, patience is the watchword. Patience and careful study. And maybe a little luck.

CHAPTER 8

How Foreign Markets Work

Sometimes foreign markets don't work. No question about that. Sometimes the U.S. market doesn't work so well, either. And when it acts up or breaks down, investors tend to get out and stay away for a while. A year and a half after Black Monday, for example, brokers are still trying to entice individual investors back to common stock ownership. So one suspects that fear of market failure keeps many U.S. investors from becoming global investors. That, and fear of the unknown. In this chapter we look at the workings of markets around the world, to put their risks in perspective and make them seem less alien.

A View of Market Failure

In response to the massive selling pressure of Black Monday, Hong Kong simply closed its stock market for four days. Investors were temporarily trapped in positions they desperately wanted to abandon. Ever since, Hong Kong officials have been struggling to straighten out the ensuing mess and institute reforms to ward off future disasters. The sad story will undoubtedly have a positive ending.

Black Monday was very hard on U.S. markets, too. True, they stayed open for the duration. The government wasn't jeopardized nor did recession ensue. But our markets were scarcely a model of grace under pressure. A year later, two-thirds of the claims that investors filed against broker-dealers during the crisis remained unresolved.

Investors around the world have been fleeced by "boiler room" operations based in European countries such as Switzerland, where one can sell securities without a license. From their temporary quarters, unregistered brokers send out sophisticated-appearing newsletters with market analysis and recommendations. Then they follow up with phone calls touting the recommended stocks at inflated prices. Sometimes they claim an impending takeover is pushing up the value. After customers buy, the brokers typically drop out of sight, leaving angry investors with worthless securities. Officials in more than forty countries are trying to track down these scamsters.

Even legitimate markets sometimes fail. During the hey-day of high oil prices, a market called the Souq Al-Manakh (Souq) arose and flourished in Kuwait as a vehicle for mar-keting shares of regional companies. The fuel that kept the market hot was oil money. Then the oil cartel came apart and prices dropped. In August of 1982, as bulls in the United States began their historic stampede, the Souq collapsed, nearly taking Kuwait down with it. The market has never reopened.

Some markets work—but either not fast enough or too fast. The ISE lets paperwork pile up unconscionably, ac-cording to Colin Grimsey of Chase Manhattan Overseas Bank Corp. (Chase), in London.[1] Grimsey, at a conference of international securities administrators in Switzerland in May of 1988, also complained about Hong Kong's require-ment that trades settle within 24 hours. Unreasonable, Grimsey says. And he finds Australia is equally unreason-able for refusing to specify any settlement date. And then there's Spain. After a year in Madrid, Mr. Grimsey claimed, Chase remained unable to discern any definite settlement system. One presumes Grimsey was therefore unable to tell whether the Spanish require unreasonable promptness, as in Hong Kong, or allow unreasonable latitude, as in Australia.

Markets are manipulated. All of them. They always have been. The degree of manipulation varies with time and place. But every securities market contains sellers looking for ways to inflate prices, buyers seeking methods of deflating prices, and brokers churning accounts unjustifiably to generate commissions. And of course a few in each category are moving heaven and earth to get insider information.

Governments, too, manipulate financial markets. And not just the governments of emerging countries. Remember the "Gang of Seven" industrial nations that manipulate currency markets, and the exchange officials that, according to Tim Metz in *Black Monday*,[2] manipulated the Major Market Index and DJIA stocks to save the NYSE on the terrible Tuesday after Meltdown Monday. The idea of a totally free market can be very scary, especially when the market is going into free fall.

An Old Familiar Story

You can't compare things that are completely different, of course. And, for all their local peculiarities, stock markets have a lot in common wherever you find them. You buy a stock; you hold a stock; you sell a stock. It's the beginning, middle, and end of a story told around the world. Like a much-repeated rumor, however, the story has many subtle variations from place to place. In this section, we'll look at each of the steps in stock ownership and discuss some of the ways those steps differ internationally. Here are the steps:

Buying the security
Effecting the trade
Confirming the trade
Settling the trade
Holding the security
Selling the security

Entering the Order

Usually one begins with an order to buy immediately at the best available price. This is a "market order," and it can be done on any exchange—in English. On most exchanges, other types of orders are possible as well, and are sometimes desirable. A common alternative is the limit order to buy at a specified price under the current market price. Some orders specify a particular time: at the close of the market, for example, or at the opening. Other obvious variables include size. Will the market accommodate large orders efficiently? This usually doesn't pose a direct problem for individual investors, of course—but it can be, and on October 19 was, a problem for mutual funds suddenly deluged with investors wanting to redeem their shares. Can you purchase or sell an "odd lot" without paying a higher commission? (Odd-lot sizes vary considerably, as we have seen, from exchange to exchange.) And, for your bearish and daring moods, can you sell short? Not in Tokyo, where you may not enter an order for a sale of securities you don't own.

Effecting the Trade

After you enter an order, it has to be carried out. Intermediaries in the marketplace are, or ought to be, useful in that process. If you enter a market order with a U.S.

broker, you have a right to expect virtually immediate execution at the quoted price. And this holds both for exchange-traded securities and for OTC securities tracked by NASDAQ.

Other markets may not be so speedy or so reliable. This is especially devastating if you are prevented from selling a rapidly deteriorating stock for one reason or another. On exchanges with few shares trading, you may simply be unable to find a buyer. And most of the world's exchanges trade far fewer shares than the big three—Tokyo, ISE, and the NYSE. Some exchanges, moreover, impose certain trading limits that may prevent your sale. We've noted already the problems in Taipei, which limits price changes to 3 percent per day in each listed security. In practice, this means that only so many investors per day—none, on some days— can get out of undesirable positions.

The Zurich exchange, though it has no limits on price movement, has problems with speedy execution of larger trades. As a consequence, institutional investors have begun trading their Swiss portfolios on the ISE in London, which allows foreign listings, does a high-volume business in Swiss shares, executes trades electronically, and provides a haven from Swiss transaction taxes.

The Swiss market suffers, too, from a paucity of research—a problem that affects individuals more than institutions, which can afford to do their own research. Whoever does the research, however, will find that the Swiss require less financial disclosure than the United States does. Moreover, Swiss companies often maintain secret reserves. All of this reduces an investor's chance of making wise investment decisions.

Confirming and Settling the Trade

After you have entered an order, and your broker has found someone to take the other side, you, as the investor, will want some confirmation of your oral contract with the broker. In the United States, you should receive immediate, verbal confirmation of a market order followed by written confirmation of the size, price, and date of the trade. Virtually every market requires that investors receive written confirmation.

Of course you don't really complete a deal until you "settle up": until, that is, the seller hands over evidence of ownership and the buyer pays. That's the "settlement," and markets are expected to provide more-or-less efficient and affordable mechanisms to carry it through. But settlement systems aren't necessarily as developed as trading systems. Moreover, settlement takes place in the native language, not in English. In some countries—Portugal, for example— potential settlement problems are so severe brokers refuse to take orders for that country's securities.

In the United States, trades settle in five business days. So do trades in the Euromarket. On the ISE in London, however, settlement requires a fortnight. Hong Kong, as we noted in the beginning of this chapter, attempts to settle trades within 24 hours—using hundreds of messengers to make the necessary deliveries. This cumbersome system is one of the reasons the market closed on Black Monday: too many trades, not enough messengers. By 1990 Hong Kong plans to have electronic settlement.

With multinational banks and broker-dealers branching into all regions, the worldwide trend will be toward uniform, electronic settlement systems. But significant differences remain. As the forces of the marketplace apply new pressures, inadequate systems will break at their weak points. In 1987, for instance, the Brussels exchange seemed to provide a solid, if undervalued, market—until a number of Eurosecurities dealers simultaneously discovered its potential. Under the ensuing deluge of trades, the system unexpectedly broke.

Holding the Security

Once the trade settles, the stock belongs to you. In the United States this means a certificate will be printed for every 100 shares or fraction of 100 shares that you own. Not long ago it was standard practice for investors to take possession of these certificates and store them in a safe-deposit box—if not in a drawer, a mattress, or canister in the backyard. These days it's rather rare for investors to possess certificates, though you can do so if you want. Instead, certificates are held by the Depository Trust Corporation (DTC). The nominal owner of your securities, the one registered on the books of the issuing company is the DTC. DTC records indicate ownership by your brokerage firm. The firm, in turn, records your name as the actual stockholder. Under this system, the stock is said to be held "in street name." That's street as in Wall Street, indicating the nominal ownership of the securities by your broker through DTC.

If you wanted to handle a transaction without a broker, you'd probably want to follow the former custom of acquiring the certificates yourself. When you wanted to sell the stock, then, you would have to sign the back of each certificate and have the signature properly verified. Then new certificates would be created in the current owner's name.

As we mentioned in chapter 4, there are some advantages to holding certificates—especially foreign certificates—yourself. If you don't think your foreign broker is properly insured, or if you want to receive dividends, proxies, and reports directly from the company, then have the certificates shipped to you. Unfortunately, some countries—Austria, for example—require that certificates remain within their borders. If you hold stock in a Japanese company, you can take delivery of the certificate, but you can't vote your shares unless you appoint a Japanese proxy—usually your Japanese broker. There is, of course, a fee for that service.

During the holding period, the nominal owner is on the company's mailing list. If the nominal owner is you, therefore, you receive dividend checks directly. If not, they go to your broker, who forwards them to you. Some companies will reinvest your dividends in stock if you request that service. In some cases, the company or your broker will deposit your dividends directly into a bank or brokerage account. The named owner of the stock will also receive annual and interim reports and proxy ballots for voting on membership to the board of directors and a limited number of other matters. In the U.S., these documents are forwarded to the actual or beneficial owner.

Selling the Security

Eventually, you want to sell, which brings us full circle—for at this point your interests are very similar to those of a buyer. You have to enter an order, trade, and see the trade confirmed and settled. As a seller, you want precise and current price information to help you make the most profitable deal. You want a buyer there immediately to snap up your shares at a good price. And you want to retain as much of your profit as possible—which means keeping a lid on commissions, fees, markups, and taxes.

The larger and more liquid the market, the better chance you have of meeting your goals as a seller. Exchanges generally have listing requirements to ensure that each stock meets some reasonable standard of liquidity. As you can see from appendix 3, the Japanese market and the London ISE now outrank both the NYSE and NASDAQ in the United States, and Toronto ranks between the NYSE and NASDAQ. As you move down the list, however, the capitalization of the exchanges shrinks rapidly. After the top 10, you're looking at less than 1 percent of market capitalization per exchange. Moreover, liquidity can be a problem even on the largest exchanges when many investors rush to sell at the same time. That, of course, was one of the unpleasant discoveries of Black Monday in 1987. And you run into even more danger when buying stock in smaller companies on smaller exchanges. This could be an issue in the Thai market, for example, where foreign investment is limited to a percentage of outstanding shares in each stock. Having bought up all available shares of major companies, foreign investors are now filling up their quotas in the smaller, inherently less liquid stocks.[3] On the other hand, these smaller companies may offer much greater growth potential in an expanding market. And the foreign shares of major companies are trading at a premium, which is good for sellers.

Other problems have been mentioned before. One is the unexpected increase in capital gains taxes, which occurred in Taiwan in 1988 and was compounded by the difficulty investors had selling in the market with limits on daily price changes. Another is the effect of limitations on conversion of native currency into dollars, a policy in effect in Italy at this writing.

Over the longer term, sellers' difficulties should become less significant. If the markets expand in smaller countries such as Thailand, liquidity should increase. The pressures of merging into the European Community by 1992 will force countries such as Italy to remove restrictions on currency exchange. Growth of the global market should, in fact, have the same effect everywhere. Moreover, as a long-term investor, you will be bothered by these inconveniences far less than short-term speculators who must move very quickly to make their profits. The long-term foreign investor can afford to delay selling during a crisis that will last only a week, a month, or even a year.

Where Markets Come From and Where They're Going

Let's back up now and put present similarities and differences between markets into historical perspective. Markets may be more or less tightly regulated, but they do not spring fully formed from the minds of legislators and rule makers. They are shaped, too, by the desires of those who want to buy, sell, or issue stock. How close they come to fulfilling those desires depends on available technology, the ingenuity of traders in adapting that technology, and the strictures of government or industry regulators (who respond to the needs of various players in the market, political pressure, and established principles of justice). There is a marketplace of markets, so to speak, in which buyers and sellers shop around for the market that best suits their needs. That shopping is now, at least potentially, a global process.

The Origins of Markets

It all starts between a buyer and a seller. First, you have a company willing to trade ownership for investment capital. They sell stock. The owners of that stock need a way of transferring ownership to other buyers. Forces emerge to shape an organized marketplace. You have sellers who want easy access to buyers. You have buyers who want solid information about which companies are best to own. Journalists and analysts begin to follow the prices of stocks, and pressure grows[3] to improve communications. Investors want to know how they are faring in the growing markets.

The market organizes. Brokers and dealers set up shop to mediate between buyers and sellers. For a commission, they bring buyers and sellers together. Or they buy the securities from the sellers, mark them up, and sell to the buyers. Either way they satisfy the mutual demands of the two trading parties. And they become a third force in the market. Though they make trading easier — routine, uniform, predictable — they are also a potential threat. Buyers believe brokers favor sellers. Sellers suspect brokers give the edge to buyers. Both buyers and sellers complain that commissions and markups are getting out of hand.

Somewhere along the line brokers and dealers may organize and begin to trade through common facilities at one location. Medieval marketplaces and trade fairs, historically speaking, were the starting point for securities markets — for at those gatherings someone would have to perform financial functions, including currency exchange and lending.

Later, in the great cities such as London and New York, brokers and businessmen would convene daily in coffeeshops and alleyways to talk about buying and selling. The stockbrokers and stockjobbers (dealers) in London congregated along Change Alley in the neighborhbood of the Royal Exchange. By 1697, in fact, parliament had begun to regulate the young industry: the market was visible enough to be in disrepute for alleged insider trading and price manipulation. Similarly, in the United States, brokers gathered in coffeehouses or along the streets to swap rumors and exchange shares of stock. In New York, the center of government until the capital moved to Philadelphia in 1792, this activity took place along Wall Street near Trinity Church and the home of Alexander Hamilton.

Exchanges and Other Changes

When the coffeehouses became overcrowded, exchanges were born. In New York, it began with the legendary Buttonwood Agreement of 1792, when the brokers operating under the trees and in the coffeehouses along Wall Street established certain common rules governing their

activities. The resulting NYSE, at first an upstart competitor of the Philadelphia Exchange, has since survived
challenges from many other trading places. The nearby
Amex, on good days back in the 1950s, traded as many
shares as the NYSE. Now it is dwarfed by the NYSE, as
you can see from the relative space devoted to each in your
newspaper. These days the premier U.S. Exchange has a
strong competitor and a nagging rival in what is known
as "the fourth market"—OTC, that is, trading that occurs
off the exchange and without intermediation between large
institutions. There are also other exchanges in the United
States—regional stock exchanges, for example, the Chicago
Board Options Exchange (CBOE), and the commodities exchanges in Chicago.

The ISE in London, though it has changed names and
locations since its inception, dates back to the mid eigh-
teenth century, when stockbrokers (who arrange trades as
agents) and stockjobbers (who buy and sell stocks as prin-
cipals) banded together to acquire their own building and
charge dues to keep out the riffraff. Their first meeting place
was the New Jonathan's—a 1748 reincarnation of Jonathan's coffeeshop, which had burned down. The brokers and
jobbers simply hung a sign over the door proclaiming that
the New Jonathan's was "The Stock Exchange." In 1801 it
closed for a time and reopened as "The Stock Subscription
Room," a temporary home for trade while masons constructed the new stock exchange in Capel Court, a building that lasted a century and a half. Then technology
advances forced the construction of a new and more modern facility, which sufficed until the next revolution in technology precipitated the "Big Bang" in 1986.

Over in Vienna, an exchange was founded in the 1770s
to trade government bonds. Stocks were not introduced
until the early nineteenth century. The world's largest exchange, located in Tokyo, dates back to 1878. It, too, was
founded to trade bonds. Within a few years, the Tokyo

Exchange shared its business with over 130 other Japanese trading places, a number that has since been reduced to 7. As the marketplace grows, exchanges tend to grow with it, sometimes by consolidating. Hong Kong, for example, merged its 4 exchanges into 1 in 1986. In appendix 3, you can read the basic statistics for 61 of the world's current stock exchanges.

It's growing noticeably quieter on the floor of the NYSE. Computers are replacing people as traders. The silence is even more dramatic in the ISE. Not long after the Big Bang revolutionized London's financial industry in late 1986, the British began to wonder if they might have to find new uses for their stock-exchange building. Trading had moved from the "pitches" on the exchange floor to dealers' rooms full of telephones and terminals. In the meantime, British brokers lost the right to fix commissions—a change that had come to the United States a decade earlier; the barriers separating various financial institutions were removed; nonmembers of the exchange, including foreign firms such as U.S. banks, were allowed 100 percent ownership of members; and corporations, including foreign firms, were allowed to join the exchange. The old London Exchange merged with the new International Securities-Regulatory Organization (ISRO), representing the Eurosecurities dealers based in London, to become the ISE.

The history of stock exchanges is, clearly, a wild and woolly story, full of dramatic transformation. The forces that propel these changes range from human greed through technological innovation. Such a volatile brew naturally invites, as we saw in connection with the coffeehouse trade in London, government regulation. And as soon as there are rules and regulators, they become a force to reckon with, an impediment to making money at a rate satisfactory to the more inventive and imaginative—not to say acquisitive—investors and brokers. They find a way around the rules; the government (or its designated regulators) makes more rules; investors invent more ways to circumvent the rules. Meanwhile more players participate; the number of shares traded mushrooms; communications technology advances; and one day the marketplace looks quaintly irrelevant. Under the pressure of new forces, it collapses. And the whole process lurches forward into a new era.

Which is pretty much where we are at present: in midlurch, with new investment instruments, new trading systems, new exchanges, new multinational companies, new regulations, new communications technology, and new international trade arrangements almost daily revolutionizing the way we think about investment. All of which leads us to wonder what the future markets of the world will offer to the global investor. One can only look at present trends, of course, and extrapolate. The U.S. and Eurosecurities markets are most instructive examples of the way the future is shaping up.

Exchanges and the Future: The U.S. Model

An exchange is a place where buyers and sellers, or their representatives, gather to exchange securities of specified companies. To qualify for listing on the NYSE or the nearby Amex, a company must want to be listed and must meet certain requirements regarding capitalization and interest in its stock. In addition there must be a truly national market for its shares. Stocks with only a regional market may be listed on the Boston, Philadelphia, Cincinnati, Midwest, or Pacific exchanges. The New York exchanges also handle a small percentage of the secondary bond market and some stock options.

Instruments other than stocks tend, at least in the United States, to trade on exchanges other than stock exchanges. While the NYSE and other stock exchanges do handle some stock options, for example, the CBOE specializes in stock options, and also lists options on a variety of market indexes and certain government securities. All foreign currency options, however, trade on the Philadelphia Exchange (PHLX). CBOE made a bid for that market in the mid 1980s, but was unable to wrest it away from the PHLX. The trading of commodities is handled by specialized exchanges, such as the New York Cotton Exchange, the New York Commodities Exchange, the Chicago Mercantile Exchange, and the CBT. Commodities trading is also separately regulated.

Since exchanges restrict their listings, they offer in return certain benefits to attract those companies they like. One such benefit shows up in your daily paper, *The Wall Street Journal, Barron's,* and elsewhere in the media: U.S. exchanges keep track of price changes, trading volume, and various other essential information. Through the media, they provide that information to the public. In addition, they actively regulate the industry, under the jurisdiction of the SEC, which was established by Congress during the Depression.

Taken together, the stock trading on U.S. exchanges is called the "exchange market" and is of primary importance in terms of its capitalization and trading volume. Next in importance is the so-called OTC market. Traditionally a refuge for those companies too small to qualify for exchange trading, the OTC market has grown in recent years to list more stocks than the NYSE. On particularly active days it may also match the exchange in trading volume. Usually, however, it trades substantially fewer shares, and it is still much smaller than the NYSE in its total capitalization. Though there is some dispute about the origins of the OTC market, it certainly dates back more than a century, when the typical OTC trade occurred in a bank and was literally transacted over a counter.

These days there is no counter in OTC trading. There is also no exchange building, trading floor, or other physical location where all trades must take place. Instead, there is a nationwide network of security dealers called market-makers, who continuously buy and sell securities using the telephone and computers. Really, they operate in an over-the-phone or through-the-computer market. Unlike brokers, who act as agents in trades and are compensated by a commission, market-makers actually buy securities in their own accounts and sell them to customers. In between buying and selling, they of course mark up the price of the security, and that markup is their compensation. The price a market-maker will pay to buy a security is called the bid; the selling price is called the offer or ask price.

Exchange vs. OTC Trading

Between them, the U.S. exchange market and the OTC market illustrate the two basic ways of trading securities all around the world. So let's look briefly at the way they work, beginning with the exchange market as illustrated by the NYSE.

Each stock listed on the exchange is assigned to a specialist in that stock. All Honda ADRs, for example, are traded by one specialist firm operating on the floor of the exchange. The firm acting as Honda's specialist places a representative, also known as the specialist, at a spot on the trading floor called a post. The specialist at the post keeps track of orders to buy and sell Honda in the "specialist's book," which of course is no longer a book but a computer program.

When you call your broker and place an order for Honda, in other words, you aren't buying stock from the firm employing your broker. You are, instead, asking the firm to have its representative on the exchange go to the Honda specialist's post and find a seller. The specialist on the floor operates as both a broker and a dealer, acting as your broker's broker in some cases, buying and selling stock in its own account in others. The specialist, in fact, is an authorized market manipulator, responsible for buying and selling stock in its own account when that seems necessary to stabilize the market and prevent wide price swings. In chapter 6, we discussed the possibility, raised by Tim Metz in *Black Monday,* that NYSE specialists had manipulated the market upward on October 20, 1987, to keep it from collapsing altogether.

The preceding description of the exchange market is the traditional view and is accurate enough to use in contrasting the exchange and OTC approaches to trading. The important point here is that the specialist system used by the stock exchanges is controversial enough that many companies eligible for NYSE listing—good examples are MCI Telecommunications Corporation (MCI) and Apple—choose to trade over the counter instead. Such companies contend that the exchange system of assigning each stock to a single specialist is inferior to the OTC system of multiple market-makers in each stock. Having multiple dealers should, at least in theory, provide price competition. It should also provide greater liquidity in each stock—more shares trading at any given time.

These potential benefits of OTC trading have emerged only as communications improved. In the past, filling an OTC order at the best available price might require calls to several market-makers—a slower procedure than operating through one specialist. Computers changed all that. Now an OTC stockbroker simply enters the ticker symbol for a security into a computer, and quotes from all market-makers appear on the screen. At least, it works this way for the major OTC stocks tracked by NASDAQ, which inaugurated computerized listing and trading in 1971. As of October 1988, NASDAQ was providing computerized data on 5,287 securities, with 2,910 of those included in its especially thorough National Market System (NMS). At that time, total NASDAQ volume for the year equaled 75 percent of the NYSE's and more than 12 times that of the Amex.[4] And it isn't just listings that have been automated, but the entire trading system—execution, settlement, and confirmation.

In NASDAQ's first year, market watchers were startled to discover that 2.2 billion shares of stock traded in the system. Until that time, no one had a solid idea of the market's size. Seventeen years later, OTC volume averaged about 120 million shares a day. In capitalization, the OTC is now the fifth-largest stock market in the world, behind Tokyo, the ISE, the NYSE, and the TSE. (See appendix 3.) In number of listings, it far outranks the NYSE's 1,600 securities—as you can see in your daily paper or, better yet, in *Barron's*.

Although the statistics eloquently speak for the advances made in OTC trading, the exchange market has also been transformed by the communications revolution. From telegraphs to telephones and from computers to satellites, communications advances haved shaped the exchange market. The largest Wall Street firms are known even today as "wire houses," a term dating back to the time when only the largest broker-dealers had nationwide branches linked together by rapid communications systems. In fact, without the telephone and telegraph, the very notion of centralizing the nation's trading at one location would have made little sense.

Now, of course, it's computers that are doing the changing. For example, the computers in the NYSE's Designated Order Turnaround (DOT) system execute small orders— 5,099 shares before the exchange opens, 2,099 after. The specialist at his or her post receives notice of these executions about the same time as the broker and customer do. Since the DOT system reduces the amount of paper that must be carried about on the floor, exchange volume has been able to multiply in recent years without forcing the exchange to add seats or expand its floor space.

How much has the exchange grown? In August of 1982, the investment world was astonished when the first surgings of the long bull market pushed trading up to 100 million shares a day for the first time in history. Now 100 million shares is a slow day on the exchange—indeed, it's a slow day on NASDAQ—and handling volume twice that size presents no difficulties. On Black Monday, the trading frenzy resulted in a 600-million-share day, and that was a problem. But the exchange officials believe their systems will soon be able to handle a billion shares of trading in a day.

When DOT began, many feared that only the largest firms would be able to afford the computers necessary to survive the advent of automated trading. Though the costs of automated trading have proved a problem for midsized firms, they seem to be adapting. Small firms actually benefit from another sort of computerization: they are able to do all their bookkeeping on a PC.

And the trend continues. Satellites provide the means to link the nationwide market of the United States with the rest of the world. Telephone and television can reach anywhere in the world—and one can now dial a U.S.-based broker from the Virgin Islands using an 800 number. A computer-based exchange in Bermuda is a present possibility. Information about currency exchange, interest rates, stock prices, option premiums, and the cost of contracts for future delivery of crude oil, cocoa, cotton, and all other commodities can go anywhere in the world with no more than a hiccup's worth of lag time.

The barriers to constructing a global marketplace no longer are technical. Politics stands in the way. Cultural differences interfere. Language is a problem. The need to register foreign securities with the SEC limits access to the U.S. marketplace. Withholding taxes and limits on currency exchange are obstacles in some places. But the technological potential is here.

211

As things stand, U.S. trading systems are used around the world, with variations and, sometimes, with different names. (OTC trading in London is sometimes called the *third-tier route*, for example. A firm known in the United States as a dealer or market-maker—one that buys and sells stocks as a principal rather than arranging trades as an agent or broker—would be called a stockjobber in the United Kingdom.) Some London broker-dealers use the NASDAQ market in the United States to trade U.S. securities. And, when the United Kingdom revamped the London stock market in 1986, it used the NASDAQ system as a model—leading to the virtual abandonment of the exchange floor. Even in countries with almost all trading done on exchanges—Canada, Hong Kong, and Japan, for example— the exchanges are, like the NYSE, increasingly computer-supported. Whether exchange trading or a worldwide market-maker system carries the future, electronic technology will surely be the key providing entry into a global market.

Eurosecurities

The most striking example of the pressures that shape and alter securities trading is provided by the Eurosecurities market, which emerged as a major force in the 1960s. Actually, its exact date of birth is a matter of controversy among those who watch it. Some say it began in 1963, when Italy floated a dollar-denominated bond to finance the development of a highway called the Autostrada. Whether or not this was the first true Eurosecurity, it had the characteristics that define that unique instrument. Namely, it was a security issued in one country (Italy), denominated in another country's currency (U.S. dollars), and underwritten by a group of European financial services firms. When all three of those elements exist, you have a Eurosecurity.

Why the 1960s? For one reason, U.S. dollars were

accumulating in Europe and had to be put to some use. And why were dollars migrating away from home? Europeans were selling bonds with higher coupons than those available in the United States. So investors were putting their dollars into European securities. Once the dollars got to Europe, they were likely to stay there, because European banks were able to offer higher interest rates on dollar deposits than were U.S. banks. Subject to FRB requirements, the U.S. banks couldn't compete.

In an attempt to staunch the outflow of dollars, the Kennedy administration levied the interest-equalization tax (IET), so called because it aimed to equalize the yields of U.S. and European securities by imposing a penalty of 15 percent on dollars invested out of the country. That raised the effective price of European securities high enough to offset their more attractive interest rates.

The episode obviously provides a marvelous example of the way markets compete for investment capital—and how government gets involved. It also shows that investors are not easily foiled in their search for access to a more lucrative market. One way around the IET was to invest dollars that were already outside the U.S.—emigrant dollars, you might call them, or, in the name actually coined at the time, Eurodollars. And overseas banks, especially those in London, had for years been accumulating U.S. dollars that had arrived on vacation, so to say, and never returned home. Some of those dollars came in as aid: the Marshall Plan sent many a dollar abroad. Some came in as direct investment. In those days, dollars made a good reserve currency for the banks. Stable. Strong. Predictable. So the bankers made them welcome.

And there they were when U.S. investors needed them, already resident in Europe and so not subject to Kennedy's tax. But U.S. borrowers circumventing the IET weren't the only ones attracted to Eurodollars. So were many European bond issuers. They were accustomed to raising U.S.

capital through syndicates of U.S. investmant bankers, who would go to Europe for dollars instead of to a bank at home. This was a good use of Eurodollars, no doubt, but a clumsy system for acquiring them. U.S. underwriters really didn't know the European investment markets as well as, say, British, German, or Swiss bankers. One of the innovations of the Eurobond market was its use of an international consortium of underwriters in place of the U.S. firms used traditionally. And there you have the three elements of Eurosecurities trading in place: issuers from abroad, U.S. dollars (or a third-country currency), and European underwriters.

The typical Eurobond deal works like this: a corporation or government in Europe or Asia decides to issue a security. It selects a lead underwriter that puts together a syndicate including British and German banks. A Swiss bank enters, acting for an unidentified buyer who pays with dollars from a European source. The unnamed buyer receives interest and principal repayment also in U.S. dollars from a European source. None of the dollars passing between buyer and borrower ever enters the United States. None of the dollars is subject to U.S. taxes. But that anonymous buyer could very well be a U.S. investor—say, a multinational corporation with foreign subsidiaries.

For most of the 1960s, the system worked flawlessly. All participants were sophisticated and well capitalized, and none lamented the total absence of any regulations governing this borderless community of expatriate capital. Toward the end of the decade however, things began to unravel. Some major defaults hit the market, a few of which made Bernie Kornfeld and Robert Vesco instantly infamous. And the market's clearing system went lame.

Despite the fact that the market short-circuited the United States for tax purposes, it still sent its paperwork through New York banks. Unfortunately, this was before the days of automated clearing systems, back when sorting out receipts and certificates was a hands-on occupation. Also unfortunately (in a sense), the United States was, at the time, enjoying a bullish run on its stock markets. The influx of Euromarket paperwork combined with a blizzard of receipts and stock certificates from U.S. transactions to put the clearing system into the deep freeze. Piles of unsorted receipts and undelivered bonds drifted into basement vaults on Manhattan island, while underwriters awaited their checks and Swiss bankers went without their bond certificates. And these were bearer bonds, you understand—the kind fringed with coupons to clip and return if you want your interest sent to you. Locked up in the basement, the coupons went unclipped. So those nameless buyers represented by those punctilious Swiss bankers went without their interest checks—sometimes for as long as a year and a half.

As a consequence, the United States modernized its clearing system. Bearer bonds have gone out of fashion. Now bonds are just registered to the owner, who receives interest without having to clip coupons. But Euromarket trades don't clear through New York anymore. To bypass the paper jam, Morgan bank set up a clearing firm in Luxembourg called, of course, Euro-Clear Clearance System (Euro-Clear). The French, thinking a little competition would not hurt the clearing business, set up a rival firm called Cedel SA (Centrale de Livraison de Valeurs Mobilières), also in Luxembourg. At present, both firms are electronically linked and operating prosperously in Luxembourg. As of 1987, Cedel was using sophisticated clearing procedures to process trades in stocks and bonds, handling payment in 22 of the world's currencies.

Trades may clear through Luxembourg, but the heart and home of the Euromarket is London, where, for decades —centuries, really—bankers have been involved in foreign trade and finance. In 1979, London moved to full convertibility of its currency. By the middle of the 1980s, banks from other European countries had set up their trading branches in London to take advantage of the currency market there. All this activity, involving sophisticated institutional traders, remained largely unregulated and completely independent of the London Stock Exchange. And, as the market developed in complexity, it included instruments other than straight debt. In the beginning—back there in the early 1960s—the Euromarket was truly the Eurobond market. It was also strictly a Eurodollar market. But before long it added other expatriate currencies: Euroyen, Eurodeutschemark, and even Eurodinar bonds were issued when the dollar was out of favor. Later, Eurobonds began trading with warrants, thus giving the market some equity experience. Gradually, the major British stocks began to move off the London exchange to trade in the nearby Euromarket, along with issues from the United States, Germany, Switzerland, and the Netherlands—much to the consternation of the abandoned exchanges and countries.

And there's another lesson in the competition that shapes markets.

By the time the United Kingdom got around to modernizing the London Exchange in 1986, the biggest British stock, ICI, was trading 62 percent of its volume in the Euromarket. Meanwhile, the Eurosecurities traders banded together into the International Securities Regulatory Organisation (ISRO), with a staff of three persons, and challenged the London Exchange's right to be considered the only game in town. Since then, the two organizations have merged into the world's second-largest securities market, the ISE. The ISRO acceded to the regulatory authority of the London Exchange, but by virtue of the power of their members, the ISRO dominates the board. And the whole organization more closely resembles (by conscious design) the U.S. OTC market than a traditional exchange.

Meanwhile, there's talk, as we noted earlier, of turning the old exchange building into a shopping mall.

Summary

World securities markets vary in all sorts of ways—in safety, efficiency, accessibility to foreign investors, relative freedom from manipulation, size, liquidity, and degree of regulatory oversight. Yet the differences between markets, one suspects, are doomed to eventual extinction.

Like other businesses, stock markets compete. If investors—especially mammoth, multinational institutional investors—don't like the local market, they'll either go elsewhere or they'll build their own market. In the battle to dominate Wall Street, for example, the NYSE has buried its one-time rival, the neighboring Amex. The PHLX and the CBOE (which didn't exist until 1973) were recently locked in combat over the market for options on currencies. The CBT and the Mercantile Exchange are hometown rivals battling each other for dominance in their markets.

While the exchanges weren't looking, the idea that trades must take place in some central location became obsolete. In the meantime, the OTC market (which of course doesn't involve counters at all) tied its nationwide network of dealers together by telephone and computer and hustled into the modern world. In fact, when the London Exchange transformed itself in 1986 in the process known as the Big Bang, it took its cue from NASDAQ, the automated quote system of the OTC market, not from the venerable exchange on Wall Street. And why did the London Exchange undergo such radical reform? Because it had suddenly found itself dwarfed by the Eurosecurities market set up by multinational corporations as an alternative trading place.

As of now, the future of trading seems to belong more to the computer screen than to the exchange floor; and one can project a time when all markets will be hooked together in some version of NASDAQ with thousands of international issues, both debt and equity, tracked constantly in price, trading volume, and perhaps even financial ratios. Along with this apparently decentralizing tendency, however, one should note a contrary movement, visible in the evolution of the Eurosecurities market. Instantaneous communications and the bridging of country borders has played midwife to the global conglomerate. Advanced and available technology could make everyone a broker. Or it could turn the business over to multinational megacorporations. As it is, large trades by U.S. international investors are sometimes accomplished in the ISE after the NYSE closes. Though the securities involved may be listed on the NYSE, the massive trades never show up in the market's prices—which may help to temper the effects of a Black Monday–style meltdown. All is handled cheaply and efficiently in London's new market, using the NYSE closing prices.

Similarly, there is now a growing "fourth market" in the United States, a network of institutional investment managers who trade directly with one another through two computer networks: Instinet Corporation's Crossing Network and Portfolio System for Institutional Trading (POSIT). These systems exist primarily to facilitate the enormous trades of institutions adjusting their portfolio positions. Though they take place entirely off the exchange, their prices may be established by reference to the closing prices on the NYSE. These systems charge no admission or membership fees, reduce commissions as trades grow larger, and answer (as the exchanges are quick to note) to no regulations. Though these off-exchange systems are now relatively small, perhaps 1 percent of exchange volume, they have the feel of the future about them—a global future, an electronic future, a future that belongs to unsleeping giants who never have to eat and are at home both everywhere and nowhere.

218

Endnotes

1. Clive Wolman, "Settlement policies criticised by Chase banker," *Financial Times*, May 17, 1988, p. 1.

2. Tim Metz, *Black Monday* (New York: William Morrow, 1988).

3. "Investors Seeking to Profit from Thailand's Boom Are Often Limited to the Stock of Smaller Concerns," *The Wall Street Journal*, April 24, 1989, p. C10.

4. These figures come from NASDAQ *Notes*, vol. 10. no. 11 (November 1988).

CHAPTER 9

Bullish on the World

Investing is an act of faith. For decades, stockbrokers have been telling their prospects that buying stock is putting your money on the U.S. economy—over the long term. And they can point to those wonderful charts that show the trend of stock prices steadily rising over the years. On the average. In the short-term, of course, prices rise and fall. But on the average, U.S. economic history has been a tale of continuous growth. We've had a lot of catching up to do, since our forebears overseas got off to a head start.

Now it may be time for the rest of the world to catch up to us. While that happens, the growth rates in other countries will outpace our own. Global investing, then, becomes an act of faith in the larger world. Table 9–1 compares estimated rates of growth in industrialized and newly industrialized countries and shows what would have happened to $1,000 invested in those markets from 1978 to 1988.

Needless to say, these figures represent average growth. The economies that are surging ahead are usually led by particular companies, whose rate of growth may be double that of the country. As a nation's general wealth grows by 100 percent, in other words, particular companies

Table 9–1. World Growth Rates (estimated), 1978–88

Country/Region	Growth Rate (Annual)	Growth of $1,000 in 10 Years
U.K. & Europe	2%	$1,243
U.S.	3%	1,384
Japan	6%	1,898
Newly Industrialized Countries	8%	2,332
China	10%	2,853

may quadruple in size. Think of the part that steel and automobiles played in the development of the United States, for example, or of the importance of electronics to Japan.

Consider, too, the aspects of an industrializing country that are most likely to grow. Will the phone company be hooking up telephones to millions of households that never before could afford such a luxury? Will construction companies be contracting to develop highways? Will an emerging middle class be spending money on clothes, cars, and entertainment for the first time? These are the kinds of clues you need to locate the most profitable companies in the fastest-growing economies.

Development and Stock Markets

As countries expand economically, they need to draw in capital from countries with surpluses of money. Stock markets are one magnet they use to attract such investment capital. And countries therefore pursue policies designed to make the magnet more powerful. They open the markets up to foreign investment, legislate reasonable taxes on dividends and gains, modernize clearing and settlement procedures, and develop regulations that ensure fair treatment for all investors.

Peace Is Good for Investors

Peace and prosperity are two sides of a coin. Nothing is more important for economic growth than peace. War diverts a country's people, creativity, and material resources away from economic development into the cause of destruction. Fortunately, there are today large areas of the world that have been free of war for three or four decades and seem anxious to continue their peaceful development.

The EC, for example, is pulling down the trade barriers between nations that are, after all, ancient enemies. Moreover, Western Europe now seems willing to accept overtures to economic cooperation from Eastern Europe. Hungary, for example, has a solid trade agreement with the EC giving it equal trading rights with the twelve member nations. Poland, too, has applied for recognition as a trading partner. Even the Soviet Union is exploring the possibility of such an agreement.

Along the Pacific Rim, talks are in progress between North and South Korea. Vietnam is withdrawing troops from its neighbor states. Thailand is flourishing and there is, at last, hope for peace in Kampuchea. After a recent tour of the region, Prime Minister Hawke of Australia reported that new markets are blooming in the killing fields, as one newpaper article phrases it.[1]

There are, of course, more ominous developments around the world. The Middle East continues to be a source of tension. Israelis and Palestinians walk a thin, high wire between war and peace—and the rest of the world is divided in support of one side or the other. Iran, free of its long war with Iraq, seems ready to turn its guns against the West. Even in South Korea dissent is turning more violent. South America staggers under its debt. Central America is split by revolution and, in many cases, at odds with the United States. South Africa defies the

223

UN-sponsored boycott and relations between blacks and whites remain bitter. There were the tanks in Tienanmen Square. We will not cry peace where there is no peace. The millennium is not upon us. But large areas of the world are free of war, and the countries there are ready to benefit from the investment of your dollars.

International Trade

Growing agreement among nations to institute more favorable trade and tariff policies draws the world closer together and, incidentally, erects another barrier to war. Citizens of trade-linked nations find more peaceful outlets for competitive desires, channeling their energies into activities that foster economic development, higher national income, and greater financial well-being. Nations compete for improved living standards rather than territory and military dominance.

It's true that fierce economic competition may seriously harm industries that are not competitive or not protected. Yet the overall outcome of economic struggle is to create wealth rather than to destroy it. Like Olympic athletes, all nations may improve as the level of competition increases generally.

Long-Term and Short-Term Effects on Stock Prices

Over the long term, stock prices will rise along with the changes outlined above. Widespread economic growth, greater international trade, closer economic ties among nations, continued absence of war, and the increased importance of stock markets in raising development capital all tend to boost the values of foreign stocks in your portfolio.

Like the course of true love, however, the adventure of global investment does not necessarily run smooth. Along the way, most investors experience significant pain. You may select a company that loses its markets to vigorous competitors. Your choice of country or currency may give you first-hand experience of the pitfalls we described in chapter 5. You may simply buy the right stock at the wrong time. Even stocks of successful companies in growing economies drop in price from time to time. If you buy just before the drop, you may wait months or years for your gains to begin. Like lovers' quarrels, these episodes hurt. Like lovers' quarrels, they should not lead to disenchantment with your long-term goals.

Global investors have to be long-term investors, at least at present. As we indicated in chapter 5, international information flow is too thin and slow a trickle to float the unstable craft of short-term speculation. As a long-term investor, you must be willing to suffer through temporary setbacks patiently, meanwhile maintaining your faith that peace, international cooperation, and continued global growth will carry you toward your long-range objectives.

On to Part Three

To help you reach your long-term goals as a global investor, we have assembled a variety of current information into the appendixes composing part 3 of this book. There you will find charts of markets and currencies, a brief refresher course in currency exchange calculations, information on the composition of most of the world's stock markets, addresses of international broker-dealers, a copy of the foreign tax credit form, and a list of information sources to keep you up to date.

The rest is up to you. We have suggested that at least 10 percent of your portfolio should be invested outside the United States. May that 10 percent grow so successfully that it constitutes an ever larger fraction of your net worth. Your success, after all, will be a reflection of worldwide economic development and harmony, which are long-range goals for us all.

Endnotes

1. Geoff Kitney, "Markets Bloom in Asia's Killing Fields," *Financial Review*, February 6, 1989.

PART III

GLOBAL DATA

A P P E N D I X E S

The following four appendixes are here to help you make decisions. The information in them is current as of the summer of 1989. Things change. The list of sources (Appendix 4) and the Bibliography that follows will guide you to references that will help keep you current.

Appendix 1: Market and Currency Charts

The first appendix contains ten-year and three-year charts representing stock markets in 18 countries. For many countries, there are three charts. One gives stock prices in the country's own currency; a second shows the history of the rate of exchange between the country's currency and the dollar; the third gives prices in U.S. dollars.

The long-term charts are semilog; the short-term charts are arithmetic.

The countries and their market indexes are arranged by size. Japan, the market with the largest capitalization on June 30, 1988, is listed first. Others follow with their market capitalization determining their location within this appendix. The sources and valuations of market capitalization are in appendix 3.

Appendix 2: An Easy Guide to Currency Calculations

The second appendix provides a quick reminder of how to do currency conversions. It will help you use available tables and charts to calculate a foreign stock's value in dollars, to determine the amount of a foreign stock you can buy with a given amount of U.S. money, and to find the value of a foreign stock in a currency other than dollars.

Appendix 3: Stock Exchanges, Their Addresses, and Other Information

Along with the addresses of almost sixty stock exchanges from around the world, you will find some rather interesting data about their relative sizes. Bear in mind that market capitalization—given here in U.S. dollars—changes with the currency rate. As the yen doubled against the dollar in the middle of the 1980s, for example, the Japanese stock market capitalization in dollars also doubled.

Appendix 4: Information Sources

Here you will find computer services offering information on stock prices, currencies, and market indexes. Books and periodicals are listed in the Bibliography.

APPENDIX 1

Market and
Currency Charts

Japan
A1.1 Nikkei 225, 1980–89, arithmetic
A1.2 Nikkei 225, 1980–89, semilog
A1.3 Japanese yen–U.S. dollar exchange rate 1985–89
A1.4 Nikkei 225 in U.S. dollars, 1985–89

United Kingdom
A1.5 FTSE 500, 1980–89, arithmetic
A1.6 FTSE 500, 1980–89, semilog
A1.7 British pound–U.S. dollar exchange rate 1985–89
A1.8 FTSE 500 in U.S. dollars, 1985–89
A1.9 U.K. index in Japanese yen, 1985–89, U.S. commerce department data

United States of America
A1.10 Dow Jones Industrial Average, 1980–89
A1.11 Dow Jones Industrial Average in Japanese yen, 1986–88
A1.12 Dow Jones Industrial Average in British pounds, 1986–88
A1.13 Dow Jones Industrial Average in Australian dollars, 1986–88
A1.14 Dow Jones Industrial Average in Canadian dollars, 1986–88

Canada
A1.15 Toronto Stock Exchange (TSE) 300, 1979–89, semilog
A1.16 Canadian dollar–U.S. dollar exchange rate, 1985–89
A1.17 TSE 300 in U.S. dollars, 1985–89

France
A1.18 CAC General, 1980–89, arithmetic
A1.19 CAC General 1980–89, semilog
A1.20 French Franc–U.S. dollar exchange rate, 1985–89
A1.21 CAC General in U.S. dollars, 1985–89

Germany
A1.22 FAZ Aktein, 1980–89, semilog
A1.23 German mark–U.S. dollar exchange rate, 1985–89
A1.24 FAZ Aktein in U.S. dollars, 1985–89
A1.25 DAX, 1988–89
A1.26 DAX in U.S. dollars, 1988–89

Australia
A1.27 All Ordinaries, 1980–89, arithmetic
A1.28 All Ordinaries, 1980–89, semilog
A1.29 Australian dollar–U.S. dollar exchange rate, 1985–89
A1.30 All Ordinaries in U.S. dollars, 1985–89
A1.31 All Ordinaries in Japanese yen, 1986–88
A1.32 All Ordinaries in British pounds, 1986–88

Italy
A1.33 Banca Comit Italia, 1980–89, arithmetic
A1.34 Banca Comit Italia, 1980–89, semilog
A1.35 Italian lira–U.S. dollar exchange rate, 1985–89
A1.36 Banca Comit Italia in U.S. dollars, 1985–89 (Times 100)

Switzerland
A1.37 Swiss Bank Index, 1980–89, arithmetic
A1.38 Swiss Bank Index, 1980–89, semilog
A1.39 Swiss franc–U.S. dollar exchange rate, 1985–89
A1.40 Swiss Bank Index in U.S. dollars, 1985–89

Spain
A1.41 Spain, 1988–89

Sweden
A1.42 Sweden, 1988–89

A1.1   Nikkei 225, 1980–89, arithmetic

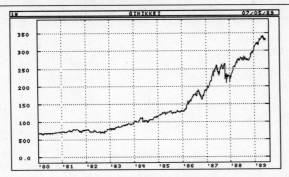

A1.2   Nikkei 225, 1980–89, semilog

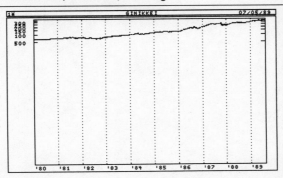

A1.3   Japanese yen–U.S. dollar exchange rate, 1985–89

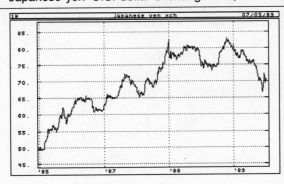

A1.4 Nikkei 225 in U.S. dollars, 1985–89

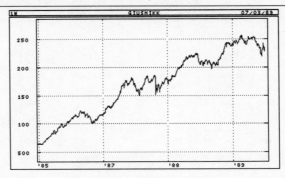

A1.5 FTSE 500, 1980–89, arithmetic

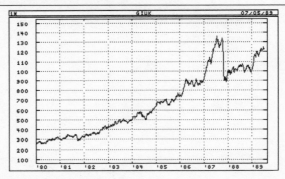

A1.6 FTSE 500, 1980–89, semilog

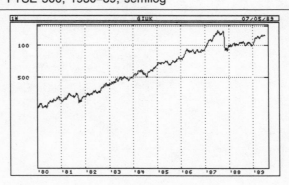

A1.7 British pound–U.S. dollar exchange rate, 1985–89

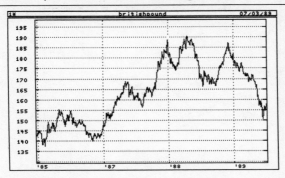

A1.8 FTSE 500 in U.S. dollars, 1985–89

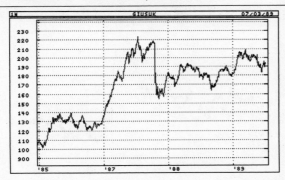

A1.9 U.K. index in Japanese yen, 1985–89

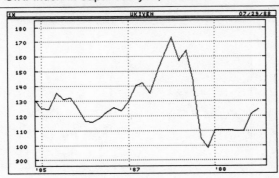

A1.10 Dow Jones Industrial Average, 1980–89

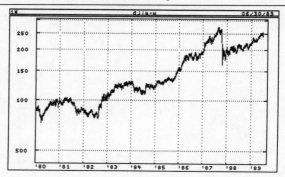

A1.11 Dow Jones Industrial Average in Japanese yen, 1986–88

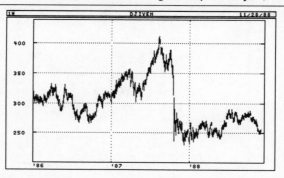

A1.12 Dow Jones Industrial Average in British pounds, 1986–88

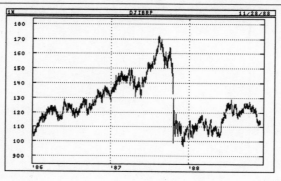

A1.13   Dow Jones Industrial Aveage in Australian dollars, 1986–88

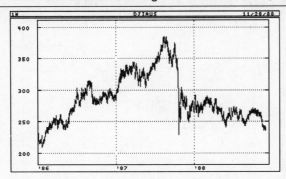

A1.14   Dow Jones Industrial Average in Canadian dollars, 1986–88

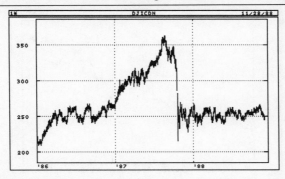

A1.15   Toronto Stock Exchange (TSE) 300, 1979–89, semilog

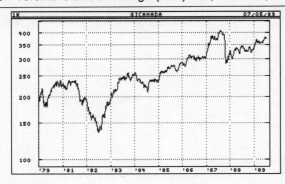

A1.16 Canadian dollar–U.S. dollar exchange rate, 1985–89

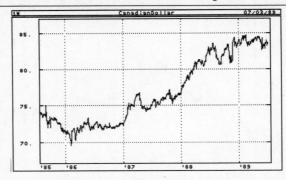

A1.17 TSE 300 in U.S. dollars, 1985–89

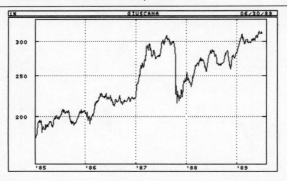

A1.18 CAC General, 1980–89, arithmetic

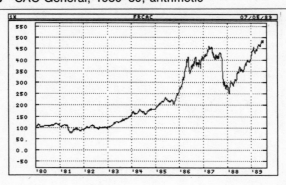

A1.19 CAC General, 1980–89, semilog

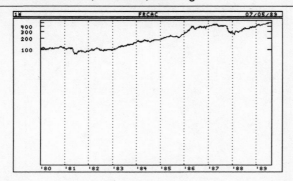

A1.20 French franc–U.S. dollar exchange rate, 1985–89

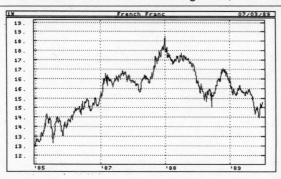

A1.21 CAC General in U.S. dollars, 1985–89

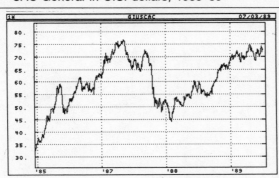

A1.22 FAZ Aktein, 1980–89, semilog

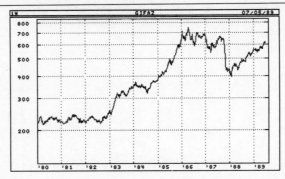

A1.23 German mark–U.S. dollar exchange rate, 1985–89

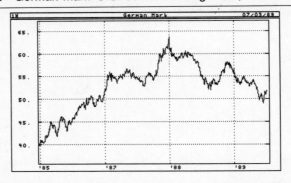

A1.24 FAZ Aktein in U.S. dollars, 1985–89

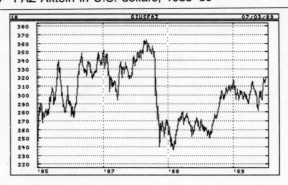

A1.25 DAX, 1988–89

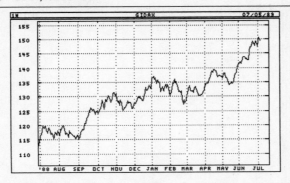

A1.26 DAX in U.S. dollars, 1988–89

A1.27 All Ordinaries, 1980–89

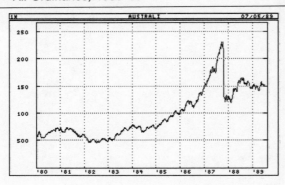

A1.28   All Ordinaries, 1980–89, semilog

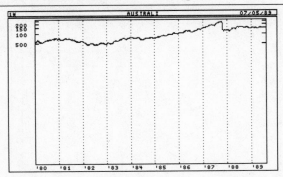

A1.29   Australian dollar–U.S. dollar exchange rate, 1985–89

A1.30   All Ordinaries in U.S. dollars, 1985–89

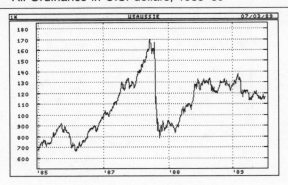

A1.31 All Ordinaries in Japanese yen, 1986–88

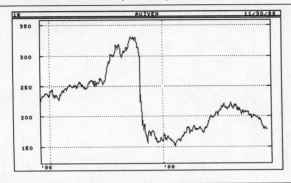

A1.32 All Ordinaries in British pounds, 1986–88

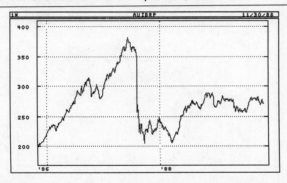

A1.33 Banca Comit Italia, 1980–89, arithmetic

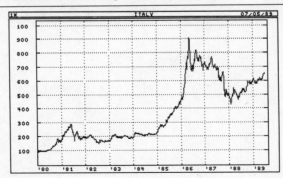

A1.34 Banca Comit Italia, 1980–89, semilog

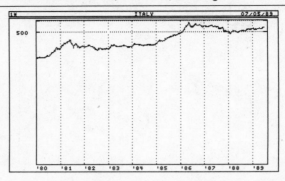

A1.35 Italian lira–U.S. dollar exchange rate, 1985–89

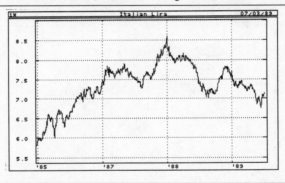

A1.36 Banca Comit Italia in U.S. dollars, 1985–89 (Times 100)

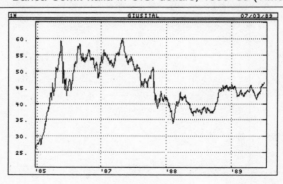

A1.37 Swiss Bank Index, 1980–89, arithmetic

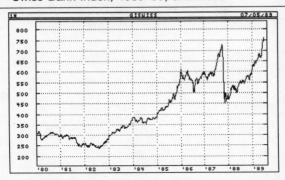

A1.38 Swiss Bank Index, 1980–89, semilog

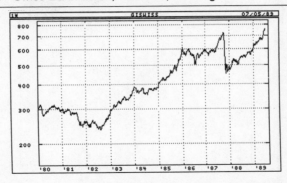

A1.39 Swiss franc–U.S. dollar exchange rate, 1985–89

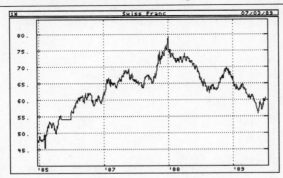

A1.40 Swiss Bank Index in U.S. dollars, 1985–89

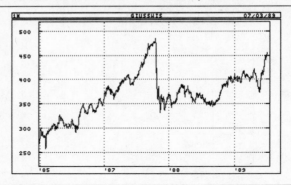

A1.41 Spain, 1988–89

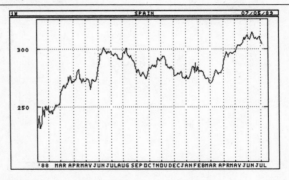

A1.42 Sweden, 1988–89

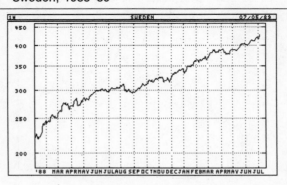

A1.43   Hong Kong, 1980–89

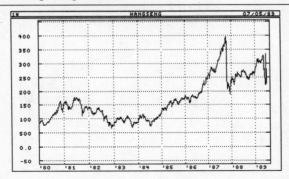

A1.44   Hong Kong dollar–U.S. dollar exchange rate, 1985–89

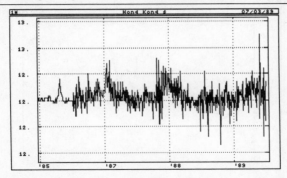

A1.45   Brussels Stock Exchange, 1985–89

A1.46 Belgian franc–U.S. dollar exchange rate, 1985–89

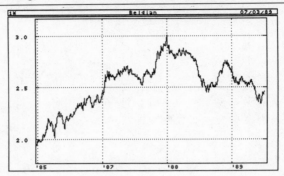

A1.47 Brussels Stock Exchange in U.S. dollars, 1985–89

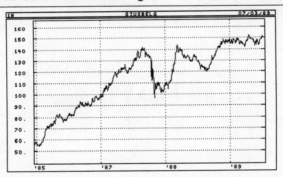

A1.48 Straits Times, 1979–89, arithmetic

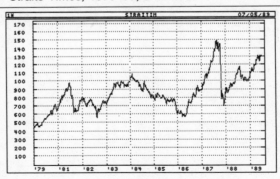

A1.49   Straits Times, 1979–89, semilog

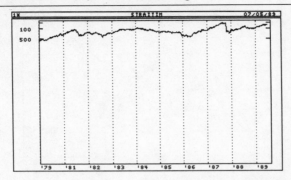

A1.50   Singapore dollar–U.S. dollar exchange rate, 1985–89

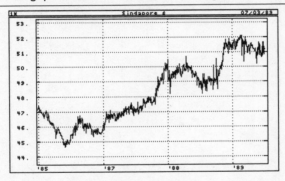

A1.51   Straits Times in U.S. dollars, 1985–89

A1.52   Finland, 1987–89

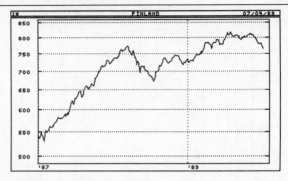

A1.53   Denmark Stock Exchange, 1987–89

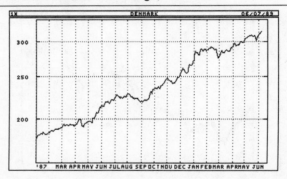

A1.54   Norway, 1987–89

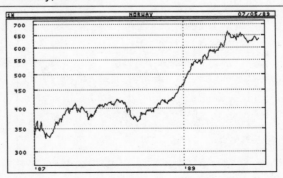

A1.55 Credit Aktein, 1980–89, semilog

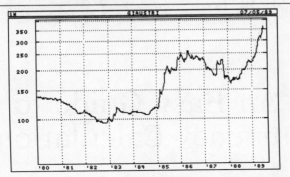

A1.56 Austrian shilling–U.S. dollar exchange rate, 1985–89

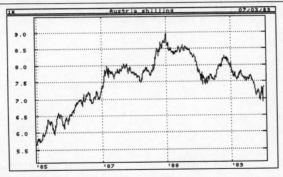

A1.57 Credit Aktein in U.S. dollars, 1985–89

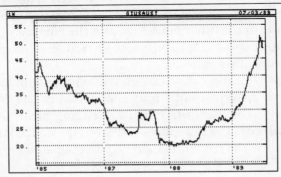

An Easy Guide to
Currency Calculations

The following two tables demonstrate the way currency exchange rates appear in *Barrons* and *The Wall Street Journal*. They list the same countries, include cash and forward contracts, and have the same format. They list U.S. dollar equivalents in the other currency, and the currency per U.S. dollar. Both show the most recent price and the time the quotes were obtained.

The *Wall Street Journal* chart, which appears first, displays a Friday quote and the previous day's quote (Thursday). The *Barron's* chart appearing after the *Wall Street Journal* chart displays the day's quote (Friday) and the quote for the previous Friday. Otherwise, the information is identical.

Table A2–1. Exchange Rates from *The Wall Street Journal*

April 24, 1989

The New York foreign exchange selling rates below apply to trading among banks in amounts of $1 million and more, as quoted at 3 p.m. Eastern time by Banker's Trust Co. Retail transactions provide fewer units of foreign currency per dollar.

| | U.S. $ Equivalent | | Currency Per U.S. $ | |
Country	Fri.	Thurs.	Fri.	Thurs.
Argentina (Austral)	.014708	.014496	67.99	68.98
Australia (Dollar)	.7950	.8020	1.2578	1.2468
Austria (Schilling)	.07686	.07693	13.01	12.99
Bahrain (Dinar)	2.6521	2.6521	.37705	.37705
Belgium (Franc)				
Commercial rate	.02584	.02586	38.69	38.66
Financial rate	.02573	.02577	38.86	38.80
Brazil (Cruzado)	1.0101	1.0101	.99000	.99000
Britain (Pound)	1.7140	1.7170	.5834	.5824
30-Day Forward	1.7098	1.7130	.5848	.5837
90-Day Forward	1.7006	1.7048	.5880	.5865
180-Day Forward	1.6884	1.6925	.5922	.5908
Canada (Dollar)	.8435	.8445	1.1855	1.1840
30-Day Forward	.8418	.8428	1.1879	1.1864
90-Day Forward	.8385	.8399	1.1925	1.1905
180-Day Forward	.8347	.8361	1.1979	1.1960
Chile (Official rate)	.0039869	.0039869	250.82	250.82
China (Yuan)	.268672	.268672	3.7220	3.7220
Colombia (Peso)	.002777	.002777	360.00	360.00
Denmark (Krone)	.1389	.1390	7.1965	7.1920
Ecuador (Sucre)				
Floating rate	.001980	.001980	505.00	505.00
Finland (Markka)	.2414	.2416	4.1410	4.1375
France (Franc)	.1594	.1596	6.2700	6.2650
30-Day Forward	.1596	.1598	6.2620	6.2570
90-Day Forward	.1600	.1602	6.2485	6.2405
180-Day Forward	.1605	.1608	6.2280	6.2187
Greece (Drachma)	.006329	.006345	158.00	157.60
Hong Kong (Dollar)	.128509	.128509	7.7815	7.7815
India (Rupee)	.0636942	.0636942	15.70	15.70
Indonesia (Rupiah)	.0005737	.0005737	1743.00	1743.00
Ireland (Punt)	1.4344	1.4344	.6971	.6971
Israel (Shekel)	.5503	.5503	1.8170	1.8170
Italy (Lira)	.0007363	.0007369	1358.00	1357.00
Japan (Yen)	.007607	.007624	131.45	131.15
30-Day Forward	.007642	.007659	130.85	130.55
90-Day Forward	.007709	.007729	129.71	129.38
180-Day Forward	.007806	.007827	128.10	127.75
Jordan (Dinar)	1.8968	1.8968	.5272	.5272
Kuwait (Dinar)	3.4393	3.4393	.2907	.2907

(continued)

Country	U.S. $ Equivalent		Currency Per U.S. $	
	Fri.	Thurs.	Fri.	Thurs.
Lebanon (Pound)	.001934	.001934	517.00	517.00
Malaysia (Ringgit)	.36968	.36913	2.7050	2.7090
Malta (Lira)	2.9368	2.9368	.3405	.3405
Mexico (Peso)				
Floating rate	.0004464	.0004464	2240.00	2240.00
Netherland (Guilder) . . .	.4795	.4798	2.0855	2.0840
New Zealand (Dollar) . . .	.6130	.6125	1.6313	1.6326
Norway (Krone)	.1488	.1488	6.7200	6.7200
Pakistan (Rupee)	.05050	.05050	19.80	19.80
Peru (Inti)	.0006765	.0006765	1478.00	1478.00
Philippines (Peso)	.048309	.048309	20.70	20.70
Portugal (Escudo)	.006497	.006497	153.90	153.90
Saudi Arabia (Rival)	.2665	.2665	3.7510	3.7510
Singapore (Dollar)	.5158	.5137	1.9385	1.9465
South Africa (Rand)				
Commercial rate	.3949	.3935	2.5323	2.5413
Financial rate	.2457	.2463	4.0700	4.0600
South Korea (Won)	.0014992	.0014992	667.00	667.00
Spain (Peseta)	.008684	.008710	115.15	114.00
Sweden (Krona)	.1587	.1586	6.2990	6.3030
Switzerland (Franc)	.6125	.6142	1.6325	1.6280
30-Day Forward	.6142	.6160	1.6280	1.6232
90-Day Forward	.6178	.6197	1.6186	1.6135
180-Day Forward	.6236	.6254	1.6035	1.5988
Taiwan (Dollar)	.03723	.03723	26.86	26.86
Thailand (Baht)	.039292	.039292	25.45	24.45
Turkey (Lira)	.0004901	.0004901	2040.00	2040.00
United Arab (Dirham) . . .	.2722	.2722	3.6725	3.6725
Uruguay (New Peso)				
Financial	.001913	.001913	522.50	522.50
Venezuela (Bolivar)				
Floating rate	.02797	.02797	35.75	35.75
W. Germany (Mark)	.5411	.5414	1.8480	1.8470
30-Day Forward	.5428	.5431	1.8421	1.8410
90-Day Forward	.5460	.5463	1.8314	1.8304
180-Day Forward	.5505	.5507	1.8164	1.8156
SDR	1.30770	1.30239	0.764701	0.767819
ECU	1.12386	1.11762	. . .	. . .

Special Drawing Rights (SDR) are based on exchange rates for the U.S., West German, British, French and Japanese curencies. Source: International Monetary Fund.

European Currency Unit (ECU) is based on a basket of community currencies. Source: European Community Commission.

z—Not quoted.

Table A2–2. Exchange Rates from *Barron's*

April 24, 1989

The New York foreign exchange selling rates below apply to trading among banks in amounts of $1 million and more, as quoted at 3 p.m. Eastern time by Banker's Trust Co. Retail transactions provide fewer units of foreign currency per dollar.

Country	U.S. $ Equivalent		Currency Per U.S. $	
	Fri.	Last Fri.	Fri.	Last Fri.
Argentina (Austral)	.014708	.02094679	67.99	44.74
Australia (Dollar)	.7950	.8107	1.25786	1.23350
Austria (Schilling)	.0768639	.07604562	13.01	13.15
Belgium (Franc)				
Commercial rate	.0258417	.0255689	38.6971	39.11
Financial rate	.0257311	.02543881	38.8634	39.31
Brazil (Cruzado)	1.0101	1.0101	.99	.99
Britain (Pound)	1.7140	1.7053	.58343	.5896407
30-Day Forward	1.7098	1.7014	.58486	.58775126
90-Day Forward	1.7006	1.6938	.58802	.59038847
180-Day Forward	1.6884	1.6838	.59227	.59389476
Canada (Dollar)	.8435259	.84388185	1.1855	1.1850
30-Day Forward	.8418217	.842388185	1.1879	1.1850
90-Day Forward	.8385744	.83941912	1.1925	1.1913
180-Day Forward	.8347942	.83561131	1.1979	1.1967
Chile (Official rate)	.0039869	.00400144	250.82	249.91
China (Yuan)	.2686727	.2688172	3.7220	3.7200
Colombia (Peso)	.00277777	.00277777	360.00	360.00
Denmark (Kroner)	.1389564	.13759889	7.1965	7.2675
Ecuador (Sucre)				
Floating rate	.00198019	.00196078	505.00	510
Finland (Markka)	.2414878	.236906287	4.1410	4.1830
France (Franc)	.1594896	.15860428	6.2700	6.2962
30-Day Forward	.1596933	.15882592	6.2620	6.2790
90-Day Forward	.1600384	.15926102	6.2485	6.2530
180-Day Forward	.1605651	.15992323	6.2280	6.2530
Greece (Drachma)	.00632911	.00629722	158.00	158.80
Hong Kong (Dollar)	.1285099	.12855122	7.7815	7.7790
India (Rupee)	.06369426	.06389776	15.70	15.65
Indonesia (Rupiah)	.00057372	.00057372	1743.00	1743.00
Ireland (Punt)	1.4344	1.4215	.697155	.70348223
Israel (Shekel)	.55035773	.55035773	1.8170	1.8170
Italy (Lira)	.00073637	.00072926	1358	1371.25
Japan (Yen)	.007607	.0075633	131.45	131.99
30-Day Forward	.007642	.00761208	130.85	131.37
90-Day Forward	.007709	.00768462	129.71	130.13
180-Day Forward	.007806	.00779655	128.10	128.28
Jordan (Dinar)	1.8968	1.8968	.5272	.5272
Kuwait (Dinar)	3.43938	3.44827586	.29075	.2900

(continued)

257

Country	U.S. $ Equivalent		Currency Per U.S. $	
	Fri.	Last Fri.	Fri.	Last Fri.
Lebanon (Pound)	.0019342	.00240963	517.00	415.00
Malaysia (Ringgit)	.3696857	.36697247	2.7050	2.7450
Malta (Lira)	2.936855	2.90697674	.3405	.3440
Mexico (Peso)				
Floating rate	.0004464	.00042708	2240.00	2368.00
Netherland (Guilder) . . .	.4795013	.47427083	2.0855	2.1085
New Zealand (Dollar) . . .	.6130	.6105	1.631321	1.648001
Norway (Krone)	.1487652	.1472754	6.7220	6.7900
Pakistan (Rupee)	.050505	.05089058	19.80	19.65
Peru (Inti)	.0006765	.00069060	1478.00	1448.00
Philippines (Peso)	.0483091	.04830917	20.70	20.70
Portugal (Escudo)	.0064977	.00641641	153.90	155.00
Saudi Arabia (Rival)	.2665955	.2666	3.7510	3.7500
Singapore (Dollar)	.5158627	.51216384	1.9385	2.5575
South Africa (Rand)				
Commercial rate	.3949	.3923	2.5323	2.5493
Financial rate	.2457	.2439	4.0700	4.1000
South Korea (Won)	.0014992	.00149186	667.00	670.30
Spain (Peseta)	.0086843	.00860867	115.15	116.17
Sweden (Krona)	.158755	.15731927	6.2990	6.3565
Switzerland (Franc)	.61255	.60742270	1.6325	1.6630
30-Day Forward	.61425	.60934738	1.6280	1.6411
90-Day Forward	.61781	.61330880	1.6186	1.6305
180-Day Forward	.62363	.61965547	1.6035	1.6138
Taiwan (Dollar)	.03723008	.03705075	26.86	26.99
Thailand (Baht)	.0392927	.03921568	25.45	25.50
Turkey (Lira)	.00049019	.00049431	2040.00	2023.00
United Arab (Dirham) . . .	.272294	.27229407	3.6725	3.6725
Uruguay (New Peso)				
Financial	.00191387	.00194363	522.50	514.50
Venezuela (Bolivar)				
Floating rate	.027972	.02747252	35.75	36.40
W. Germany (Mark)	.541125	.5363825	1.8480	1.8638
30-Day Forward	.542858	.53478795	1.8421	1.8578
90-Day Forward	.546030	.54165312	1.8314	1.8462
180-Day Forward	.550539	.54680664	1.8164	1.8288
SDR	1.30770	1.29657	0.764701	0.771269
ECU	1.112386	1.10785	. . .	. . .

Special Drawing Rights (SDR) are based on exchange rates for the U.S., West German, British, French and Japanese currencies. Source: International Monetary Fund.

European Currency Unit (ECU) is based on a basket of community currencies. Source: European Community Commission.

z—Not quoted.

How Many Shares of a Foreign Security Can Be Purchased with a Specific Amount of U.S. Currency?

Steps

1. Determine the amount of local currency.
   a. Determine the amount of U.S. Currency.
   b. Determine the currency local to the security.
   c. Refer to the exchange-rate column and find the currency per U.S. dollar.
   d. Multiply the U.S. currency times the amount of local currency per U.S. dollar.
2. Determine the number of shares purchased by the amount of local currency.

$$\frac{\text{amount of local currency}}{\text{price per share}}$$

Examples

How many shares of Grand Met can be purchased for $10,000 on April 21, 1989? (Grand Met was trading at 5.54 pounds per share on that day.)

1. Determine the amount of local currency.
   a. $10,000 — amount of U.S. currency
   b. British pounds — currency local to the security
   c. .58343 — pounds per U.S. dollar
   d. $10,000 × .58343 = 5,834 pounds
2. What is the number of shares?

$$\frac{\text{number of pounds}}{\text{price per share}}$$

$$\frac{5,834 \text{ pounds}}{5.54} = 1,053 \text{ shares}$$

How many shares of ANZ on the Sydney Exchange can be purchased with $10,000 (ANZ is trading at $4.79.)

1. What is the amount of local currency?
   a. $10,000
   b. Australian dollar
   c. 1.25786
   d. $10,000 × 1.25786 = A$12,578.60
2. What is the number of shares?

$$\frac{\text{number of Australian dollars}}{\text{price per share}}$$

$$\frac{\text{A\$12,578.60}}{4.79} = 2,626$$

Value of a Foreign Security in U.S. Dollars

Steps

1. Find the value of the security in local currency.
2. Find the U.S. dollar equivalent.
3. Multiply the value of the security by the U.S. dollar equivalent.

Examples

1. Eurotunnel, a U.K. company, closed at 8.25 Friday. What is the value in U.S. dollars?
   a. The security value in local currency is 8.25 pounds.
   b. The U.S. dollar equivalent for the British pound is 1.714.
   c. 8.25 pounds × 1.714 is $14.14.

2. Wolters Kluwer, a Dutch company, closed Friday at Dfl 175.80 on the Amsterdam exchange. What is the value in U.S. dollars?
   a. The security value in local currency is 175.80 Dutch florins (guilders).
   b. The U.S. dollar equivalent for the Netherlands guilder is .4795.
   c. 175.80 Guilders × .4795 is $84.30.

Currency Cross Rates

The currency cross-rates table that is published daily in *The Wall Street Journal* can be used in the same way as the exchange-rate tables. The numbers are slightly different, because they are gathered at different times. For instance, the 3 P.M. quote in *Barron's* for the U.S.$ equivalent of a British pound is 1.714, while the late New York trading equivalent is 1.7135. The prices of currencies in the market are determined by supply and demand, and will change .0005 in a few hours, or even more.

The 1.7135 could be used for the previous Eurotunnel calculation, and the .58360 U.K. pounds per U.S.$ could be used in the Grand Met calculation.

The cross-rates table can be used to determine the value of a security holding in a currency other than local or U.S. dollars.

For instance, Wolters Kluwer is trading at Dfl 175.80. What is the value of 100 shares of Wolters Kluwer in French francs?

$$100 \text{ shares} \times 175.80 = \text{Dfl } 17,580$$
$$\text{Francs per guilder} = 3.0067$$
$$\text{Dfl } 17,580 \times 3.0067 = \text{Ffr } 52,857.79$$

**Table A2–3. Key Currency Cross Rates
(Late New York Trading April 24, 1989)**

	Dollar	Pound	SFranc	Guilder	Yen	Lira	D-Mark	FFranc	CdnDlr
Canada	1.1869	2.0338	.72794	.56898	.00903	.00087	.64209	.18924	. . .
France	6.2720	10.747	3.8467	3.0067	.04770	.00462	3.3930	. . .	5.2844
Germany	1.8485	3.1674	1.1337	.88615	.01406	.00136	. . .	.29472	1.5574
Italy	1359.0	2328.6	833.49	651.49	10.336	. . .	735.19	216.68	1145.0
Japan	131.48	225.29	80.638	63.030	. . .	.09675	71.128	20.963	110.78
Netherlands	2.0860	3.5744	1.2794	. . .	.01587	.00153	1.1285	.33259	1.7575
Switzerland	1.6305	2.7939	. . .	.78164	.01240	.00120	.88207	.25996	1.3737
U.K.	.58360	. . .	.35793	.27977	.00444	.00043	.31572	.09305	.49170
U.S.	. . .	1.7135	.61331	.47939	.00761	.00074	.54098	.15944	.84253

Reprinted by permission of *The Wall Street Journal* © Dow Jones & Company, Inc., April 24, 1989. All Rights Reserved Worldwide.

How about German marks?

Dfl 17,580 × .88615 = DM 15,578.52

How about Japanese Yen?

Dfl 17,580 × 63.030 = JY 1,108,067.40

Conclusion

The currencies and the currency cross rates are published in *The Wall Street Journal* daily. They can be used to value any security in most marketable currencies. You can easily convert your foreign interests to the currency of your choice with just a little practice.

APPENDIX 3

Stock Exchanges, Their Addresses, and Other Information

TABLE A3–1. STOCK EXCHANGES[1] (Largest to Smallest, as of June 30, 1988)

COUNTRY and Exchanges	Withheld (%)[2]	Restrictions[3] (Y/S/N)	Commissions F/N[4] %		Capitalization (US $000,000)	As % of World	Market Listings (International)	Individual Holdings %
JAPAN The Tokyo Stock Exchange 2-1, Nishombashi, Kayuto-ko Chuo-ku, Tokyo 103 Telephone: (3) 666-0141 Fax: (3) 639-5016	20	N	F	1.20–0.15	3,191,191	29	1,600	24
UNITED KINGDOM[5] The International Stock Exchange The Stock Exchange London EC2N 1HP Telephone: (1) 588-2355	0	N	N	~0.4[6]	2,659,707	24	2,656 (595)	20
UNITED STATES OF AMERICA[7] The New York Stock Exchange 11 Wall Street New York, NY 10005 Telephone: (212) 656-3000 Fax: (212) 656-5646	30	N	N	–	2,400,000	24[8]	1,681 (74)	–
NASDAQ 1735 K Street NW Washington, DC 20006 Telephone: (202) 728-8955 Fax: (202) 728-8882	–	N	N	–	374,500	–	4,700 (~200)	67

COUNTRY and Exchanges	Withheld (%)[2]	Restrictions[3] (Y/S/N) %	Commissions F/N[4] %	Capitalization (US $000,000)	As % of World	Market Listings (International)	Individual Holdings %
CANADA Toronto Stock Exchange The Exchange Tower 2 First Canadian Place Toronto, Ontario M5X 1J2 Telephone: (416) 947-4700 Fax: (416) 947-4585	25	N	—	626,924	5.6	1,700	—
FRANCE The Paris Stock Exchange Palais de la Bourse 4 Place de la Bourse 75002 Paris Telephone: (1) 4041-1000 Fax: (1) 4026-3140	25	%	F .65	244,998	2.2	888 (222)	30
WEST GERMANY Frankfurt Stock Exchange Frankfurter Wertpapierborse Borsenplatz 6 Postfach 10 08 11 6000 Frankfurt-am-Main Telephone: (69) 2197-0 Fax: (69) 2197-455	25	N	N —	186,601	1.6	741 (329)	—

COUNTRY and Exchanges	Withheld (%)[2]	Restrictions[3] (Y/S/N)	Commissions F/N[4]	Commissions %	Capitalization (US $000,000)	As % of World	Market Listings (International)	Individual Holdings %
AUSTRALIA Sydney Stock Exchange Plaza Building, Australia Square Sydney, NSW 2000 Telephone: (2) 233-5266 Fax: (2) 235-0056	30	S	N	–	164,930	1.5	1,506 (47)	10
ITALY The Milan Stock Exchange via Camperio 4 20123 Milan Telephone: (2) 805-7674 Fax: (2) 8534-4640	32.4	N	F	0.7	135,428	1.2	211	–
SWITZERLAND Zurich Stock Exchange Bleicherweg 5, CH-8021 Zurich Telephone: (1) 229-2111 Fax: (1) 211-1938	35	S	F	2.5 to 0.1	125,403	1.1	2,914 (1,105)	10
LUXEMBOURG The Luxembourg Stock Exchange Société de la Bourse de Luxembourg 11 Avenue de la Porte Neuve L-2011 Luxembourg Telephone: 447-9361 Fax: 22050	35	N	F	.8	109,894	1.1	243 (183)	–

COUNTRY and Exchanges	Withheld (%)[2]	Restrictions[3] (Y/S/N)	Commissions F/N[4]	Commissions %	Capitalization (US $000,000)	As % of World	Market Listings (International)	Individual Holdings %
TAIWAN The Taiwan Stock Exchange 85 Yen-Ping S. Road Taipei 10034 Telephone: (2) 311-4020 Fax: (2) 311-4004	N/A	Y	F	0.15	92,008	—	—	41
NETHERLANDS Amsterdam Stock Exchange Beursplein 5 1012 JW Amsterdam Telephone: (20) 523-4567 Fax: (20) 248-062	25	N	F	1.5 to 0.7	91,720	—	572 (291)	—
SPAIN The Madrid Stock Exchange Bolsa de Madrid Plaza de la Lealtad 1 28014 Madrid Telephone: (1) 589-2600 Fax: (1) 531-2290	18	%	F	0.25	88,777	—	360	—
SWEDEN The Stock Exchange Stockholms Fondbors Kallargrand 2, P.O. Box 1256 S-111 82 Stockholm Telephone: (8) 143-160 Fax: (8) 108-110	30	%	N	~0.5	81,788	—	157 (9)	20

COUNTRY and Exchanges	Withheld (%)[2]	Restrictions[3] (Y/S/N)	Commissions F/N[4]	Commissions %	Capitalization (US $000,000)	As % of World	Market Listings (International)	Individual Holdings %
SOUTH AFRICA The Johannesburg Stock Exchange Diagonal Street P.O. Box 1174 Johannesburg 2000 Telephone: (11) 833-6580 Fax: (11) 838-1463	15	N	F	1.2 to 0.2	73,147	—	680	32
HONG KONG The Stock Exchange of Hong Kong 1/F Exchange Square Central, Hong Kong Telephone: (5) 211-122 Fax: (5) 845-3554	0	N	N	~0.25	71,697	—	308	—
SOUTH KOREA The Korea Stock Exchange 33 Yoido-dong, Youngdeungpo-ku 150-010 Seoul Telephone: (2) 783-2271 Fax: (2) 782-0417	26.875	Y	F	0.9	57,007	—	~400	68
BELGIUM Brussels Stock Exchange Palais de la Bourse 1000 Brussels Telephone: (2) 509-1211 Fax: (2) 513-7275	—	N	—	—	50,535	—	340 (152)	—

COUNTRY and Exchanges	Withheld (%)[2]	Restrictions[3] (Y/S/N)	Commissions F/N[4] %	Capitalization (US $000,000)	As % of World	Market Listings (International)	Individual Holdings %
SINGAPORE Stock Exchange of Singapore 1 Raffles Place OUB Centre Singapore 0104 Telephone: (65) 535-3788 Fax: (65) 535-0985	33	S	F (min) 1.0 to 0.5	~ 42,744	—	326 (194)	25
MALAYSIA Kuala Lumpur Stock Exchange Block A, Komplek Bukit Naga Off Jalan Semantan, Damansara Heights 50490 Kuala Lumpur Telephone: (3) 254-6433 Fax: (3) 255-7463	40	S	F 1.5 to 0.5	36,760	—	292 (57)	19
BRAZIL São Paulo Stock Exchange Rua Alvares Penteado 151 01012 São Paulo SP Telephone: (11) 258-7222 Fax: (11) 36-0871	25	Y	F 20. to 0.5	26,283	—	~580	24
FINLAND Helsinki Stock Exchange P.O. Box 429, Fabianinkatu 14 00101 Helsinki Telephone: (0) 624-161 Fax: (0) 612-1548	—	S	F 1.0	26,028	—	124 (3)	35

COUNTRY and Exchanges	Withheld (%)[2]	Restrictions[3] (Y/S/N)	Commissions F/N[4]	Commissions %	Capitalization (US $000,000)	As % of World	Market Listings (International)	Individual Holdings %
DENMARK Copenhagen Stock Exchange Køpenhavns Fondsbors 2 Nikolaj Plads, P.O. Box 1040 DK-1007 Copenhagen K Telephone: (1) 933-366 Fax: (1) 128-613	—	N	N	~1.0 to 0.25	21,344	—	297 (7)	—
INDIA The Stock Exchange (Bombay) Phiroze Jeejibhoy Towers Dalal Street, Bombay 400 001 Telephone: (22) 275-860	—	Y	N	2.5 (max)	18,443	—	2,233	38
NEW ZEALAND New Zealand Stock Exchange P.O. Box 2959 Caltex Tower, The Terrace Wellington Telephone: (4) 727-599 Fax: (4) 731-470	—	%	N	2.5 to 1.0	15,208	—	387 (154)	—
NORWAY Oslo Stock Exchange Oslo Bors, P.O. Box 460 Sentrum 0105 Oslo 1 Telephone: (2) 423-880 Fax: (2) 416-590	—	%	—	—	13,090	—	137 (6)	22

COUNTRY and Exchanges	Withheld (%)[2]	Restrictions[3] (Y/S/N)	Commissions F/N[4]	Commissions %	Capitalization (US $000,000)	As % of World	Market Listings (International)	Individual Holdings %
KUWAIT Kuwait Stock Exchange P.O. Box 22235 Safat 13083 Telephone: 242-3130 Fax: 240-125	—	Y	—	—	12,577	—	—	—
ISRAEL Tel-Aviv Stock Exchange 54 Ahad Ha'am Street Tel Aviv 65543 Telephone: (3) 627-411 Fax: (3) 662-704	—	S	—	—	10,975	—	~280	—
IRELAND Irish Stock Exchange 28 Anglesea Street Dublin 2 Telephone: (1) 788-808 Fax: (1) 776-045	—	N	N	1.65 to 0.5	9,525	—	191 (3)	21
THAILAND Securities Exchange of Thailand Sinthon Building 132 Wireless Road Bangkok 10500 Telephone: (2) 250-0001 Fax: (2) 254-3040	—	%	—	—	9,451	—	~90	43

271

COUNTRY and Exchanges	Withheld (%)[2]	Restrictions[3] (Y/S/N)	Commissions F/N[4]	%	Capitalization (US $000,000)	As % of World	Market Listings (International)	Individual Holdings %
PORTUGAL Bolsa de Valores de Lisboa Praça do Comercio 1100 Lisbon Telephone: (19) 879-416 Fax: (19) 864-231	–	N	F	0.6	7,403	–	149	–
AUSTRIA Vienna Stock Exchange Wiener Borsekammer Wipplingerstrasse 34 A-1011 Vienna Telephone: (222) 534-99 Fax: (222) 535-6857	–	N	–	–	7,001	–	170 (51)	–
CHILE Bolsa de Comercio de Santiago Calle la Bolsa 64 Santiago Telephone: (2) 698-2001	–	N	–	–	6,031	–	202	–
MEXICO The Mexico City Stock Exchange Bolsa Mexicana de Valores Uruguay 68, Mexico DF 06000 Telephone: (905) 510-4620 Fax: (905) 521-8009	–	–	–	–	~4,000	–	309	58

COUNTRY and Exchanges	Withheld (%)[2]	Restrictions[3] (Y/S/N)	Commissions F/N[4] %	Capitalization (US $000,000)	As % of World	Market Listings (International)	Individual Holdings %
GREECE Athens Stock Exchange 10 Sofokleous Street Athens 10559 Telephone: (1) 321-3930	—	N	—	3,569	—	120	—
PHILIPPINES The Manila Stock Exchange Prensa St. Cor Muelle de la Industria Binondo, Manila Telephone: (2) 408-866 Fax: (2) 471-125	—	%	—	3,427	—	140	—
PAKISTAN Karachi Stock Exchange Stock Exchange Building Stock Exchange Road Karachi Telephone: 241-3361	—	%	—	2,147	—	403 (363)	20
NIGERIA Nigerian Stock Exchange P.O. Box 2457 Stock Exchange House 2-4 Customs Street Lagos Telephone: (1) 660-335	—	N	—	1,996	—	188	99

COUNTRY and Exchanges	Withheld (%)[2]	Restrictions[3] (Y/S/N)	Commissions F/N[4] %	Capitalization (US $000,000)	As % of World	Market Listings (International)	Individual Holdings %
TURKEY Istanbul Stock Exchange Rihtim Caddesi No. 245 Karakoy, Istanbul Telephone: (1) 152-4800 Fax: (1) 143-7243	—	N	—	1,668	—	556	30
IRAN Tehran Stock Exchange No. 521, Taghinia Building Saadi Avenue 11447 Teheran Telephone (21) 311-149	—	—	—	1,550	—	—	33
KENYA Nairobi Stock Exchange P.O. Box 43633, Nairobi Telephone: 727-640 Fax: 729-349	—	Y	—	444	—	72	—
TRINIDAD AND TOBAGO Trinidad and Tobago Stock Exchange 65 Independence Road Port of Spain, Trinidad Telephone: (809) 625-5107 Fax: (809) 627-4696	—	Y	—	316	—	—	15

COUNTRY and Exchanges	Withheld (%)[2]	Restrictions[3] (Y/S/N)	Commissions F/N[4] %	Capitalization (US $000,000)	As % of World	Market Listings (International)	Individual Holdings %
PERU	—	Y	—	183	—	—	—
Bolsa de Valores de Lima							
Pasaje Acuna 191, Lima							
Telephone: (14) 286-280							
Fax: (14) 337-650							
ECUADOR	—	Y	—	—	—	32	34
Stock Exchange of Quito							
544 Amazones Avenue and							
Jeronimo Carrion, Quito							
Telephone: (2) 526-805							
NEPAL	—	Y	—	39	—	—	—
Securities Exchange Centre							
P.O. Box 1550							
Dillibazar, Katmandu							
Telephone: 4-11031							

1. Data is given by country or, where applicable, by exchange.
2. For nonresidents, as a percentage of dividends.
3. Y: Restrictions apply; S: Some restrictions apply; N: no restrictions. % limits.
4. Fixed (F) or negotiated (N); maximum or minimum indicated where applicable.
5. Some of these numbers are estimates. For instance, Singapore reports a combined stock and long-term bond total for their market capitalization. All other countries report the equity separately. So, I used 2-year-old figures for equity and debt, found 31% of the total to be equities, and applied that to the 1988 figure. All estimates of this nature are indicated with the symbol ~.
6. The U.K. second place appears to be a result of the required reporting of equity sales by the Eurosecurity dealers. They were not required to report until the regulations under the Big Bang were effective. Their reporting moved the U.K. from a definite third place, about 17% in 1987, to a market capitalization greater than the NYSE.
7. The U.S. Capitalization that includes both the NYSE and NASDAQ is slightly larger than the U.K. market, but less than 1% larger.
8. The market capitalization of the three largest countries is 77% of the world's stock-market capitalization; of the 10 largest 92%; and of the 20 largest, over 98%. Remember, smaller markets are more volatile and less liquid than larger markets. Some of the international markets with the greatest newspaper coverage are relatively small. They can grow faster as their countries can grow faster than the larger industrialized nations, but the growth may not be a steady advance. And their stock markets may reflect the fluctuations.

SOURCE: Institutional Investor, March 1989.

A P P E N D I X 4

Information Sources

As yet, no single publication brings the global investor an overview of daily news and data as the *Wall Street Journal* and *Investor's Daily* do for the domestic investor. Nor is there a weekly similar to *Barron's*. Of course those three fine publications bring you bits and pieces of the foreign news and data, so you can start with them. The *Financial Times* probably has the broadest international stock market data. Far and away the best magazine for the global investor, arguably the best magazine in English, is *The Economist*. The standard publications you probably already read — *Forbes* and *Fortune,* for example — are also very helpful.

Beyond those basic English-language sources is a wide variety of publications covering specific countries or regions, sometimes in English, sometimes not. You would have to be a library to afford them all.

Of increasing significance are computer resources that provide data on stocks, markets, and currencies. Once you subscribe to them, you can update your database daily and convert the information into charts and graphs of varied complexity and analytical refinement. We have used some of those resources to make the charts in this book. You will find their names and addresses in the following list of information sources, along with the domestic and foreign publications we found indispensable to our research.

U.S. Publications

Newspapers

The Wall Street Journal, 400 Burnett Road, Chicopee, MA 01021.

Investor's Daily, 1941 Armacost Avenue, Los Angeles, CA 90025.

Barron's, 400 Burnett Road, Chicopee, MA 01021.

Chicago *Tribune*.

Minneapolis *Star Tribune*.

New York Times.

Magazines

Forbes, 60 Fifth Avenue, New York, NY 10011.

Fortune, Time & Life Building, Rockefeller Center, New York, NY 10020-1393.

Institutional Investor, 488 Madison Avenue, New York, NY 10022.

Intermarket, 11 S. LaSalle Street, Suite 3100, Chicago, IL 60603.

Manhattan, 420 Lexington Avenue, New York, NY 10170.

Technical Analysis of Stocks and Commodities, 9131 California Avenue SW, Seattle, WA 98136-2551.

Wall Street Computer Review, Two World Trade Center, New York, NY 10048.

Non-U.S. Publications

Newspapers

Australian Financial Review, Box 506, GPO, Sidney 2001, Australia.

Financial Times, Bracken House, Cannon Street, London, EC4 P4BY.

International Herald Tribune, 181 Avenue Charles-de-Gaulle, 92200 Neuilly-Sur-Seine, France.

Magazines

Asian Finance, Hollywood Centre, 233 Hollywood Road, Hong Kong.

The Economist, 25 St. James Street, London SW1A 1HG, United Kingdom.

Financial Weekly, 14 Greville Street, London EC1N 8SB, United Kingdom.

Investors Chronicle, Greystroke Place, Felter Lane, London EC4A 1ND, United Kingdom.

Personal Investment, 392 Little Collins Street, Melbourne 3000, Australia.

NZ Financial Review, Basconds, Ltd., P.O. Box 8204, Riccarton, Christchurch, New Zealand.

Computer Resources

Databases

Molly (international databases)
    Marketbase, Inc.
    P.O. Box 826
    New York, NY 10024-0826
    Phone: 800-627-5385
Australian stock market data
    Research Technology Corporation
    Level 6.58 Pitt St.
    Sydney N.S.W. 2000, Australia
    Phone: (02) 233-6822; Telex: AA75227
Warner (daily and historical financial data)
    One University Plaza
    Hackensack, NJ 07601
    Phone: (201) 489-1580; (800) 626-4634

Lotus Signal (daily financial data via radio modem)
1900 South Norfolk
San Mateo, CA 94403
Phone: (800) 726-7538

Software

MetaStock Professional (chart preparation)
Equis International
P.O. Box 26743
Salt Lake City, Utah 84126
Smartcom (communications software)
Available at any computer software store.
Microsoft Word (word processing)
Available at any computer software store.
Pagemaker 3.0 (desktop publishing)
Available at any computer software store.

Books on Computers

Microcomputer Resource Guide
American Association of Individual Investors
625 N. Michigan Avenue
Chicago, IL 60611
Investment Information Directory
Fortune
Dushkin Publishing Group
Guilford, CN 06437
Buyers Guide
Wall Street Computer Review
Two World Trade Center
New York, NY 10048

BIBLIOGRAPHY

The International Stock Market Event of October 19, 1987

Arbel, Avner, and Albert E. Kaff. *Crash*. Chicago: Longman Financial Services Publishing, 1989.

Galbraith, John Kenneth. *The Great Crash: 1929*. Boston: Houghton-Mifflin, 1988.

McClain, David. *Apocalypse on Wall Street*. Homewood, IL: Dow Jones-Irwin, 1988.

Metz, Tim. *Black Monday*. New York: William Morrow, 1988.

Sobel, Robert. *Panic on Wall Street*. New York: E. P. Dutton, 1988.

International Markets

Berryessa, Norman, and Eric Kirzner. *Global Investing: The Templeton Way*. Homewood, IL: Dow Jones-Irwin, 1988.

Fisher, Kenneth L. *The Wall Street Waltz*. Chicago: Contemporary Books, 1987.

Goldenberg, Susan. *Trading, Inside the World's Leading Stock Exchanges*. San Diego, CA: Harcourt Brace Jovanovich, 1986.

Ibbotson, Roger G., and Gary P. Brinson. *Investment Markets*. New York: McGraw-Hill, 1987.

Nix, William E., and Susan W. Nix. *The Dow Jones-Irwin Guide to International Securities, Futures, and Options Markets*. Homewood, IL: Dow Jones-Irwin, 1988.

Smythe, David. *Worldly Wise Investor*. New York: Franklin Watts, 1988.

Solnik, Bruno. *International Investments*. Reading, MA: Addison-Wesley, 1988.

Valentine, Stuart. *International Dictionary of the Securities Industry*. London: MacMillan Press, 1985.

Warfield, Gerald. *How to Buy Foreign Stocks and Bonds*. New York: Harper & Row, 1985.

The London Marketplace

Chapman, Colin. *How the New Stock Exchange Works*. London: Hutchinson Business Books, 1986.

Hamilton, Adrian. *The Financial Revolution*. Middlesex, Eng.: Penguin, 1986.

Kerr, Ian M. *Big Bang*. London: Euromoney Publications, 1986.

Lomax, David. *London Markets after the Financial Services Act*. London: Butterworth, 1987.

Wilmot, Tom. *Inside the Over-the-Counter Market in the UK*. Westport, Conn.: Quorum Books, 1985.

Markets in Europe

Kerr, Ian M. *A History of the EuroBond Market*. London: Euromoney Publications, 1984.

Meier, Dr. Henri B., ed. *The Swiss Equity Market*. Cambridge, Eng.: Woodhead Faulkner, 1985.

Stock Markets of the Middle East

Abdul-Hadi, Ayman Shafig Fayyad. *Stock Markets of the Arab World*. London: Routledge, 1988.

Darwiche, Fida. *The Gulf Stock Exchange Crash*. London: Croom Helm, 1986.

Markets of Japan and the Far East

Rowley, Anthony, *Asian Stock Markets*. Homewood, IL:
Dow Jones-Irwin, 1987.

Viner, Aron. *Inside Japan's Financial Markets*. London: The
Economist Publications, 1987.

Wright, Richard W., and Gunter A. Pauli. *The Second Wave,
Japan's Global Assault on Financial Services*. New York:
St. Martin's, 1987.

INDEX